The Naked Soul of Pimps and Prostitutes

The Naked Soul of Pimps and Prostitutes

Quincy Mack

a.k.a.

"Late the Great"

To order additional copies of this book, contact:
Xlibris Corporation
1-888-795-4274
www.Xlibris.com
Orders@Xlibris.com
45901

Contents

Foreword

Before I began this book, I find it important that a realistic political reflection should be done on the matter of a pimp and a prostitute and the people who knowingly, or unknowingly, cater to the financial support of the game—the clients!

Throughout the years, the pimp has been the most hated and misunderstood figure in the black underworld. People who don't know anything about pimps place a biased judgment upon them.

A lot of black men find they're self-disapproving of it due to the involvement of black women. However, there is no automatic dislike toward a drug dealer, who holds no discrimination to those who purchases his product—including black women. Or is there an automatic dislike toward street gang members or representatives, who can pessimistically be viewed as those who promote, uphold, and stand for something that includes black-on-black violence, which in many situations is uncalled for and unnecessary.

Or is the prostitute herself being held accountable for her reason and will to accept herself for who she is and what she does. A person will be quick to tell a pimp that he is wrong for his conduct in regards to a black woman, but will not hold rallies and protests in front of strip clubs and black porno-distributing companies to voice their opinions about black women being sexually exploited.

The most disapproving feedback that a prostitute will get is if she were to experience a phase in her life of imprisonment, where she will encounter other women talking about "I wasn't out there on the streets selling my ass".

The critical feedback that a woman receives is small compared to a man's. If a woman is sexually promiscuous and fulfills her desire to have multiple sex partners, she will critically be considered a "slut." For the ones who are equally promiscuous but receive financial benefits for it, they are critically considered a "whore," a "hoe," or an "immoral woman."

In addition to that, they are the ones who are also critically considered a "stupid bitch," by both men and women if they have a pimp. A lot of people usually think, *If a woman decides to sell her body, she should do it for herself and not have to give her money to a man to manage for her.* But what they don't realize is this: If there was no logic or purpose as to why a prostitute has a pimp, the game of pimping and hoeing would not exist.

Most people who encounter a pimp and acknowledge him as one, feel as though they're entitled to an explanation. Either to cater to their doubt or curiosity of the lifestyle. Or simply to see if they can find themselves becoming amused. And most men, when they acknowledge a prostitute as one, feel as though she owes them a shot of her services, removing any doubt of her possibly having any guidelines in her line of business.

Pimps are critically viewed as the bad guy, and all other possible misconducts between the male and female specimen are overlooked or acceptably justified. A woman being exploited by a man for his sexual benefits are so-called "all right" and is something to brag about. But the man who exploits a woman for the both of their financial benefits is looked upon as something other than an acceptable definition for a man.

The most logical testimony that one can come up with to disapprove of the conduct of a pimp is the involvement of female minors who may have been introduced or who turned out to the game at a time when their minds may have been too vulnerable to exercise long-term judgment. However, like any other exceptional circumstances, only very few pimps conduct in this manner.

Furthermore, the average age that a woman in the United States becomes sexually active is thirteen or fourteen years old. And in many situations, their virginity was consensually taken by a male that was four to ten years older than them. In addition to that, men eighteen years of age or older are not checking every woman that they encounter for a valid ID to verify them as a legal adult. So, therefore, the age difference between the male and female sexes is nothing new. It is only the negative aspect of it being involved when a pimp is involved.

In regard to a woman, particularly one who is sexually promiscuous, their mind is in a constant desire of adventure and change. A routine without change is quickly played out to them. That's why a young woman will leave her beloved household, and everyone inside of it, to go sell some pussy for a guy she just met. And that's also why no hoe is promised to any one particular person the next day and can leave at the drop of a dime for another man—regardless of how long they have been together. Women were born with the capability of hiding their feelings, to give no possible indications of their intentions.

As far as the clients, tricks, johns, and customers, the name of the game is supply and demand. If there were no one who wanted to buy pussy, it would not be a hot commodity on the market. Men pay for pussy for different reasons. Some get a thrill out of having sex with a woman they just met, and the concept of prostitution opens that door for them. Others may not receive certain sex acts from their wives or spouses, so dealing with prostitutes removes restrictions from their particular preferred sexual acts. Regardless of what their reasons are, they are the prime source of money.

In this book, there is no mention of female or madam pimps, for the simple fact that it is an alternative form of the game, not a traditional form. The term "fake ass pimp" has become as much a common reaction to someone who is initially acknowledged as a pimp, as "bless you" is to someone who sneezes! That is driven by someone's hopeful denial of the overall existence and concept of the pimp game.

This book is not a justification for pimps and prostitutes. It is rather a reality check of the most misconceived lifestyle in the underworld. There is no justification that will ever put a person's disturbed conscience of a pimp at a halt, for one simple reason: the world is a heartbreak hotel, and any other man besides a pimp is not, and will not ever accept the reality of another man having an advantage that not only ables him to have no worries about female companionship, but to also have the honor to live off the financial earnings of multiple women as well.

This book covers everything ever thought of and everything one can possibly ever think of in regards to pimps and prostitutes. Anything left out probably doesn't exist. However, let me not forget to mention this with all due respect to the game: I am only sharing what the world *should* know, not what the world *wants* to know! The depths of any game should only be acknowledged through firsthand experience, not hearsay.

Preface

First and foremost, I would like to assure that this book is not for everybody. Some of its contents may not be suitable for people with a weak stomach, soft heart, or an easily disturbed soul. Furthermore, it contains material that may only be familiar to pimps and prostitutes. The object of this book is not to encourage anyone of a foreign lifestyle to become something that doesn't actually apply to them, but rather to give the readers who are not familiar with the particular lifestyle of pimps and prostitutes a better understanding of what is usually misunderstood or misconceived.

The entertainment industry, both movies and music alike, has projected an image to the public eye to perceive pimps on the basis of a fad, a fashion statement, a universal term or reference, pimpin', comical, or success in ones hustle that opposes to a person who manages prostitutes for a living. What is also covered are the heart, the mind, and the soul of a pimp and a prostitute in a detailed aspect of how their classifications vary, as well as the evolution of their motive and the circumstances of their conducts. People who are not honestly familiar tend to voice a strong opinion in regards to pimps and prostitutes when the topic is at hand. Usually, their opinion is brought about from something they may consider an experience, or something they reflect from a movie or fictitious documents. Here, it is being presented in a nonfiction form unlike any other book ever published. It is also not designed to offend anyone of any particular creed, ethnicity, lifestyle, occupation, sexual gender, or situation at hand.

The things that had always make people wonder or caught their curiosity are the things that are specifically covered throughout these pages. As for people who enjoy entertaining ignorance, they may take this book offensively, and it should! It transgresses against ignorance with honesty, logic, and realism. Broken down into two sections—first "The Pimp," then "The Prostitute"—each section has four subchapters designed to deal with each general topic one step at a time. The subchapters are as follows: "Generally speaking," "Stereotypes, Opinions, and Myths," "The Reality," and "Final Thought."

If you fall under the criteria of one of the aforementioned in which these contents may not be suitable for, then now would be a good time to disregard any further interest in this book and allow its destination to be back in the hands you got it from. Or any other place where it would no longer be of any concern to you. But for those of you who choose to proceed with the contents of this book, this writer hopes you'll get the satisfaction of your time, along with an understanding of *The Naked Soul of Pimps and Prostitutes.*00000

The Pimp

I've come to notice that most people who fall under an occupation that begins with the letter *P* tends to stand out by what their title represents more than them being recognized as their own self. You've got the president, police, preachers, prime ministers, punks, pedophiles, politicians, prostitutes, and pimps.

Let me give you a couple of examples of what I mean: The president will be referred to as "the president" regardless of what he's doing. He can be playing golf—"The president is playing golf" would be the most expected description from an onlooker. The president will be known as just that, whether he is awake or asleep, praying or making love. Police are what they are. When a police officer dies—whether on duty, off duty, in the line of duty, or retired—best believe that the word will be out that a police is dead. Regardless of whether it's just a small bit of gossip in the neighborhood, or something someone in a middle-class, no-crime-rate suburban neighborhood picked up on the obituary section of their daily newspaper. It'll still be basically described as, "A police officer is dead." The name of the officer will be the last thing mentioned, if at all. I'm sure you understand my point as far as people with a *P*-titled occupation.

But now we go to the pimp. He is referred to by his title to any acknowledgment of his existence, with a slight chance of his mother being the only exception. You show me a person who can hold a conversation about a pimp without referring to him as one during their discussion, and I'll show you a person that lives forever. His face isn't even able to come to mind without his title being projected in the image as if it were attached to him since birth.

But the question is, who is a pimp to have recognition beyond what sometimes seems necessary by his title? Well, let's see, with the exception of other pimps, prostitutes and people who are out of a neighborhood where the activity that pimps indulge in is only a breath of fresh air away, most people are not really familiar with them, while others can't recall ever meeting one.

So during any encounter with a pimp, he will stand out and be recognized exceptionally for his unique characteristics. Some pimps are known for having a little more wit and charisma than the average guy. Many are fast talkers who know how to take control of a conversation and leave the person at the other end at a loss of words. A pimp masters the art of having women make split-second decisions and have them doing something without much thought being put into it. A woman still may not have caught on to what she finds herself doing in regards to prostitution until after a shift or two has been put in.

The next thing they wonder is, "Oh shit. How does this guy have me out here doing this and giving him all the money while I'm at it?" But by the time they build up the urge to bring it to his attention, they are finessed into remaining mentally off balanced and proceeding with the program.

Besides a pimp's communication skills, most are known to have the ability to make which will appear to be logic on whatever point they intend to get across, or a goal they're trying to accomplish. It doesn't take long for a person who ends up in some type of debate with a pimp to catch on that they can't beat him verbally. So most of the time, a person will either drop the subject or find another alternative.

Pimps are known to make it a priority to keep themselves well groomed. There are two main purposes for that: One is to be a walking statement of success in what they do. And the other—well it's kind of obvious—looking sharp is one of the many tools used in order to catch new hoes.

Besides, a hoe wouldn't want any raggedy type of dude for her to be giving her money to. Nowadays, the pimp thing has become a serious fad and is misconceived. The entertainment industry has sidetracked minds from the true meaning of a pimp like young kids miss the true meaning of Christmas and Easter. The same way those kids think that Easter is about a bunny rabbit who lays eggs with graffiti on them, or the Christmas thing being about Santa sliding his fat ass down a hot dusty chimney just to bring them some presents then hit off every other kid on planet Earth before the sun rises is the same way that pimping is being misconceived.

Who Is and Isn't a Pimp

Most people, like in the circumstances I described earlier about those who may have encountered a pimp, are the type who may be having good luck with the ladies, or they put some customized rims on their ride, or they got familiar with a couple of young cute bitches that work at a strip club (only because of their customers) and without realizing how much of a trick they are in comparison to a pimp. They're the next one to go down in history if you let them tell it.

It has been said in other published documents that there are several different kinds of pimps, but my theory opposes to that. There is only one meaning to a pimp, and that is a person, mostly a man, who lives off the earnings of a prostitute. Also being a manager of prostitutes or an agent for prostitutes—it's as simple as that. If the money in someone's pockets didn't come from a girl who went out and indulged in sex acts with strangers just to bring some money to the person that sent her, then he isn't a pimp. My advice would be to find a different title that would be more relevant to one's particular lifestyle.

That's like a Lakers fan going to a foreign country and telling everyone that he's a professional athlete from the United States, just because he doesn't expect them to know any better, and trying his luck to see if he can receive any benefits from the first sucker that bites into his bullshit.

A pimp is what it is. It seems as if it is only those who may be somewhat disturbed with the concept of pimping who feel that pimps are not entitled to a label of their own. All pimps have heard it at one time or another: "Oh, I'm kind of like a pimp myself." Or, "Man, I know some bitches that'll get down with that on my basis if I ever wanted to get into the game. That's just not my preferred hustle."

When people start saying things like that, it's usually out of a feeling of envy or spite. They refuse to see the pimp game as something that they wouldn't be capable of doing. As far as they're concerned, if it's done then they can do it. They are not going to give a pimp the credit of being the one who has a major advantage that they themselves don't possess.

In many major cities in the United States, where there are neighborhoods that have heavy drug activity; prostitution exists there as well. So most drug dealers encounter prostitutes on a constant basis. Some drug dealers see themselves as having some pimping on their resume 'cause they've done sold some drugs to a prostitute of her preference. Although they are receiving money from prostitutes' earnings, they are not "living" off a prostitute's earnings. They are rather living off the earnings of their own hustle. Just like a prostitute has purchased some of their product, so has everyone else who is an addict that comes from many different lifestyles. Therefore, for the dealer to have considered himself pimping before is totally inaccurate. Same for the fellas in the neighborhood who's experienced a prostitute that has asked them to "watch their back" while they went out to work a street. That is not pimping for these reasons.

First of all, it didn't require any skill whatsoever. Any person that a hoe chooses to give them a sense of security can meet the criteria. And besides, who's going to turn down free money? Second of all, a hoe is very street smart. So if she gives somebody the job to do the "baby-sitting-bodyguard" thing, she's going to pay you as much as she wants you to have at her discretion.

While one might be thinking he got half, or anything else that sounded good to him, the reality would be more than likely he didn't. He gets the amount she wants him to have, just like he had the job she wanted him to have.

A person who's had this experience, as far as encounters with prostitution, gets absolutely no credit forever pimping. Hanging around a pimp doesn't make a person one. Being related to pimps, whether direct family or distant, does not make a person one. A short-term experience with having a hoe or two doesn't make a person a pimp. And neither does having a prostitute as a girlfriend.

If one had the opportunities presented to him that would have jumpstarted a career as a pimp, but was not consistent and that person ended up going back to his previous hustle, then his credit is no good. It's not even worth mentioning. Throughout a person's life, there will be many different experiences in hustles that one may go through. A person who has dipped and dabbed with prostitutes getting money for them while they took care of their maintenance, but was not consistent and still wants to consider himself a pimp, is as good as a person who has done time in prison, then long after his release, he still consider himself a convict or an inmate. It just doesn't make any sense, and it's ridiculous.

Another type of individual that may believe he's a pimp and not let anyone tell him anything different would be the gentleman who has experienced, or is currently, living off a sugar mama. You know, the woman who is missing something in life so she pays a man for his company and his companionship. Well, this type of guy will try to compare himself and his situation with pimps, and call his self-running neck and neck.

The misconception is this: while the sugar mama may be letting the man she's taking care of drive her vehicle, the vehicle that a pimp is pushing is his own. While the dude is splurging and spending money that his sugar mama is allowing him to spend, a pimp is somewhere spending his own. While the dude is living off the sugar mama, who in all actuality is doing him a favor, these types of bonds are short-term and will not last.

Just as she hired him for his companionship and services, she can dismiss him as well. A solid relationship can never be developed. First of all, most women who meet the criteria to be a sugar mama are usually women who are financially settled to one extent or the other. Their self-esteem is somewhat low, and they are mostly women who are older than the man they encounter with on a client basis. Now as far as the guy, he's probably a halfway-decent-looking fellow who at least wouldn't be expected to have a hard time getting a girlfriend.

The thing with him is he may have a low self-esteem himself as far as getting a fine young girl as his woman due to situations pending in his life. He may have a criminal history that caused him to be on parole or probation, or he's just extremely cautious of ever returning to any type of incarceration. So he figures a sugar mama will be the best way for him to stay out of trouble. Or he can be the type who isn't financially set and has insecurities of a young beautiful woman accepting him for his misfortune.

So there you have it. Two people with insecurities. As a matter of fact, the sugar mama is a little surer of herself. At least, when it boils down to it, she can accept herself for being someone who pays for what she wants. But subconsciously, she knows that if her young swinger was equal to her, or doing better than her as far as financial stability, he wouldn't give her the time or day. The reality is, there's a mismatch.

So while they're in each other's presence, there's a lot of ego boosting going on. The young man does all it takes, both sexually and verbally, to set the impression upon this older half-ass (if you're lucky)-looking woman that she's the finest bitch in the whole wide world, while all along the sugar mama knows he's full of shit. But she tells herself in her mind that there's a slight possibility that he may actually mean something he says. Besides, that's what she's paying him to do. In life, you get what you pay for.

Then again, some of the guys who get their shit together from dealing with a sugar mama don't have such a low self-esteem. Not that they would think anyway. They may share their earnings that they got from their sugar mama with a more preferable type of woman who isn't even aware of his source of income. All she'll know him as is who he portrays in front of her. That's the reason why a lot of them guys get cut off from their sugar mamas. They get too big for their bridges, forget who brought them to life, and lose focus on the woman who did it.

They tend to underestimate the intelligence of their sugar mama, and start doing whatever they well please while their esteem and confidence level is high, which causes tension in their relationship. Sooner or later, both parties on each end will not be a success for him.

Now back to the matter of comparison to a pimp. The technical science of the dude who is living off the sugar mama is very similar to the science of a prostitute. Think about it. A female prostitute gets by, by renting out her time, beauty, companionship, and whatever other qualities that's an advantage for her, to those who are in desire of what their money can buy them. Now the only difference with that general scenario with the man renting out his services in that same aspect is, he's a man dealing with a female, as opposed to a female prostitute dealing with a man.

Is there any comparison to a pimp and a guy who deals with sugar mamas? Absolutely not! Gigolo may be more of a proper title for them to go by, but since that word is not all too famous for one to be self-proclaimed, while that word also represents a career, and all guys who's had experiences with sugar mamas did not try to make a career out of it, it's not really necessary to give it a title. However, it does not apply to having any credit for even pimping.

To add to the denial frame of mind that people are in when their focus is on a pimp is his classification. Everyone likes to make comments based on their personal opinion of what a "real pimp" is. And as far as they're concerned, anyone who falls short of their judgmental criteria is not a real pimp. The specifics on that will be mentioned during the next section in the "Stereotypes, Opinions, and Myths" chapter. But in the meantime, allow me to be brief on the classification and criteria of a pimp. First of all, due to the word "pimp" having only one meaning to it (which I described earlier), nothing can be taken away from one who holds that title due to the individuality in his conduct of pimping.

There can be a pimp who at one time was very successful in the game and as time went on, he developed a crack-cocaine or heroin habit that took time and effort away from his capabilities of running a large stable of prostitutes. But as high as he may get off his drug of choice, if he's down to one hoe—a stable one at that—who happens to have the same drug habit as him, and her work as a prostitute takes care of his pockets, both of their habits and all else that is covered by finances to make their well-being convenient, then guess what, that dude is still a pimp.

He may not be spoken of highly by those who are aware of his true situation, but his label still remains. That was just an example of one of the unfortunate descriptions of a pimp. I will now give you an example of one of the more successful scenarios.

Here is a man who doesn't have the misfortune of going to jail or prison, dealing with probation or parole.

He has at least five stable hoes, in which each one has been with him for more than a year. Three or four more will keep him at an average of eight or nine girls, but those three or four are constantly juggled due to the transitory of that half of his stable. He'll be nine deep one week, then another week he'll be just as deep, but with four different girls from the previous week.

All in all, his five stable ones are still there, and his daily budget doesn't really change. Even the transitorily half of his stable will be performing about as good as his long-term stable hoes, due to being properly instructed by someone of that particular pimps status, to where his intelligence in his trade got him.

While few pimps are lucky to have a car, those who are successful usually have more than one. Their hoes work on automatic without their pimp playing taxi for them. While the pimp is laid up somewhere, or simply just enjoying leisure time, his long-term stable hoes will automatically be out working and accumulating trap (money) and come in once the quota is made. Initiating new girls into his stable is only activity, an exercise, a sport. It wouldn't make him or break him if some fresh work (new girls) came along or not. A solidified foundation has already been built. Therefore, the man doesn't pimp to live; he lives to pimp.

So there, I've given you two brief examples of a pimp. The first in a low-budget form. And the other in a successful aspect. There are hundreds of different ways that a pimp operates his program on an individual basis. No two pimps are alike, like no two musicians are alike. 50 cent is a rapper, just like Kanye West is a rapper. Both share the same era with their success. Both receive their income from albums sold, and both of them are witnessed in the public eye as rappers. However, as individuals, the activities that each one of them indulges in from the minute they wake up till the minute they go to sleep are totally different.

Therefore, no one can judge who is and isn't a pimp just by observing one of his characteristics, and using that to go by. If it was left up to the world to classify who is and isn't a pimp by their opinion, then there would be no such thing as a pimp at all. All pimps from the past, present, and future have heard or will hear someone say that they're not a pimp as far as they're concerned.

Changes

Since the nineteen sixties, the face of the pimp game has changed several times. The first change was when the police and authorities decided to become involved in pimp- and prostitution-related activity, and enforced laws about them. Pimping is not legal, just in case someone wasn't sure of that. There is no tax being paid, therefore Uncle Sam isn't getting his cut. When the activity of pimping and prostitution is occurring in an area where police want to intervene in an effort to put it to a halt, they would preferably have the motive to find reason to arrest the pimp, instead of the prostitute.

Since the ratio is three prostitutes to every one pimp, the police believe that they have a chance of decreasing the prostitution activity if fewer pimps are in society. Law officials believe that pimps play a major role in women becoming a prostitute, or carrying out a career as one. However, that is only their opinion. While police assigned to prostitution related cases have a long-term experience in that field, they still fall short of the knowledge of why and what made a woman decide to become a prostitute. (That will be covered in the section of prostitutes.)

The reality of the police becoming involved in the matter is to earn stripes back at the office. The bigger the bust, the better the reputation! Any officer can go into an undercover capacity and fool the most street smart hooker out there and arrest her, but that's too simple for them. Due to the fact they probably have several of those types of arrests under their belts, it would be nothing more than something to do. The prostitute will get a citation or a warning at the least, or an overnight or short-term stay in a police station, city or county jail at the most.

While on the other hand, the pimp, predominantly a black man, has a better chance for the police to call themselves having probable cause to make more of a solidified arrest. Since 50 percent of pimps have a criminal history to one extent or the other, currently on parole or probation. Carrying a pistol for protection, whether on foot or while driving. Driving without a license or insurance. Has active warrants, which will make him incapable of making bail or bond.

So all those possibilities make a pimp more of a target for the police, instead of the prostitute. A pimp has a better opportunity at long-term success if he doesn't have a serious criminal history. Also if he keeps enough money put up for a crisis situation. The police do what they have to do as far as having a job. But as for the male officers, they are just as much a man as the next guy, and on an everyday basis they too turn dates with prostitutes. Of course on the low, but it gets done.

Another thing that brought a major change to the pimping and prostitution trade was crack cocaine. This change occurred during the late seventies, early eighties. It has made prostitutes that had pimps become less ethical, less honorable, and less loyal. It put a financial dept in the stacking money part of the game, due to having to take care of a hoe's crack habit as part of a pimp's maintenance on his managing behalf. Crack cocaine had caused the value of sex to go down.

While a bona fide hooker may tell a trick that she charges $100 for a blow job, he may look at her like she's crazy and go to a prostitute that he's dealt with before, or drive to an area where these particular caliber of women are at and get what he's looking for—for $5, $10, $15, or $20—just because the woman has a different motive from a bona fide prostitute.

These drug addict prostitutes, referred to as "strawberries" on the West Coast, have a much more simplified goal opposed to a woman working for a pimp. Their goal is to get high, and a crispy twenty-dollar bill for fifteen minutes of their services will set them straight. And as far as the ones who have crack dealers as clients, or easy access to them, that saves them from a lot obstacles that they may have had to go through to break luck, just to get what their sole purpose of working as a prostitute is—to get high!

But for those who say that "crack fucked the game up," they're wrong. A pimp is one of the most persistent kinds of figures in the underworld. His persistency will allow him to seek and find a way around any obstacle in his path; and it's done every day. Nowadays a pimp has a first preference in women that are free from major drugs—such as heroin, crystal metamphetamine, and cocaine.

The generation of bona fide prostitutes is now mostly younger women who were initially exposed to the art of prostitution, before they've been exposed to drugs. And last but not least, in the time and era of this documentation, the latest change in the game are the pimps who are, or were recently, active gangbangers. In many major cities were gang activity is heavy, there are pimps being brought about that had a first exposure to gangbanging.

So once they get exposed to the world of pimping through someone they knew, and decided to give it a try since they have had plenty of opportunities with a girl or two from around their way, that will give prostitution a try upon his request. They tend to bring their "hood mentality" to the track with them. This causes them to set a bad impression upon themselves by those who could, and would rather contribute to an upcoming pimp by any means necessary.

Some of the most successful pimps I know from the Southern California area were once active gang members before they were reputable pimps. But not to say that they didn't go through the same phases when they first began their career. A lot of pimps from that particular breed in the beginning, with their hood mentality, have had certain scandalous thoughts going through their minds when they are on the scene where there are several pimps. Some are from around the way, and others from out of town. One of the things that cross their mind is the subconscious intent to rob one of the pimps. I mean, it's obvious. If one of those same dudes from that scene on the hoe-stroll were to be seen walking through this dude's neighborhood—with all of his jewelry on, and nobody knew him—he would get robbed. So now, this potential upcoming pimp can't help but have these thoughts cross his mind while he's in the presence of a crowd of these type of dudes that would meet the criteria to be a victim in a department that the gangsta is more familiar with.

While most of the time that doesn't play out any further than the thought of a possibility, there are still misconducts that these types of potential pimps bring out on the track. For instance, when a pimp has officially knocked another pimp off for a hoe that he had, it is his responsibility to inform that hoe's previous pimp before he sees her again, that he now has possession of the hoe by his "game," plus her choice. This is called "serving another pimp the news." Now, with the gangbangers who are just familiarizing themselves in this department, their instructions may not be that tight, and whatever girl or girls that they brought out there to work may be extremely vulnerable to the approach of a seasoned pimp.

So what usually happens in that particular situation with the gangbanger who's putting forth effort to pimp but did not come fully equipped with the knowledge of the pimp game, he is not able to accept the knowledge of the girl that he brought on his terms had been got by another pimp. And what usually ends up happening is, it ends up resulting in an alternative that gangstas are more familiar with—hostility and violence. The only time it doesn't go that far in that particular circumstance is if the gangbanger-potential pimp is pulled to the side by the person who introduced him to that lifestyle, and has the logic of that scenario explained to him right away. In a case like that, the gangbanger will more than likely come to his senses for one or two reasons. One is 'cause he'll be assured that he'll be able to move another bitch under the circumstances that he moved the previous one. And two, he wouldn't want to draw embarrassment to the reputable pimp that turned him on to the game. But now, some of the guys who started out like that happened to be some of the most successful pimps of this day. To an extent, they eventually humble themselves as they grow in knowledge of the game. Then they turn some of their aggressive and ambitious ways that they use to use as a gangster into their pimping, then end up succeeding as a pimp.

Evolution

A lot may wonder where the concept of the pimp game came from. Well, I'll put it like this in general: a prostitute needs a man just like any other woman. The art of prostitution has been known to the world before the concept of pimping came about. Back in the days of slavery, here in the United States, slave owners on the plantations continuously had sex with black female slaves. Either it was done consensually or it was forced. But either way, it was done.

Now most of the women who worked out on the fields with the other slaves and stayed in second-hand shelters that they considered a home had a husband and children in most situations. In those days, the black man was not able to put up very much objection to the overseer's decisions. So that left him to become accustomed to sharing his woman with his white slave owner. So since he was already in a no-win situation, the only option that he was left with was to finesse and encourage his woman into receiving as much as she can out of their owner, so that way he can see himself getting something out of having to share his woman.

Besides, he knew he wouldn't lose his woman under these circumstances. Because the slave owner was usually a man with a family of his own, including a wife and children. So when he's having sex with a black female slave from off the plantation, he was technically cheating on his wife—and obviously she didn't know about it. Due to the laws of nature, the black man was well aware of a man's biggest weakness being his ego and his dick. (Even though the intelligence of slaves was usually underestimated.) Well, the black man exploited his woman (which was his only alternative in that situation) and stayed in her ear with motivation and encouragement to do all she can to get all she can. Then bring it back to her man out on the plantation, and let him play his position as the male dominant figure in the relationship, and let him handle everything. All situations in regards to slavery may not have been exactly like that, but that's the most common way that it happened.

So there you have it. Pimping was developed here in this country since the beginning of it. The art of it is simple. And only someone who isn't a logical thinker would have a hard time comprehending the concept of pimping.

I am going to metaphor it with the game of chess; amongst all the pieces on the board, the two most important ones are the king and the queen. The king can only make one move at a time—any direction—but he isn't going no farther than one step. Now here's the queen. Being the most powerful piece on the board, she can finesse her way behind the enemies' lines, eliminate any obstacles that may be in her path or a hassle for her king, and be the most threatening object on his force. She's out on the front line at all times, risking her life for him simply 'cause that's her king, and she's his queen. She has an advantage of making moves that he can't.

Then when she, along with all other joining forces necessary, conquer whatever opposed to them by presenting themselves as enemies. A "checkmate" is done, and the king and queen are still on top—'cause everybody played his or her position accordingly.

And to go even a little farther into the metaphor, if the queen is smart and plays her position well, she will last and contribute to a success every time. But if she isn't strong willed and doesn't know how to play her position, she will not ride out till the end for her king, and will be eliminated out of that particular episode. Only then would it be left up to the king to use the remaining of the pieces wisely, while all along he doesn't get tipped over and taken under by the game, use his tools to the fullest extent, and get another queen. There are plenty of pieces on the board that serve their purpose, but no other is like the queen.

The king is the pimp, and the queen is the hoe. And the remaining pieces on the board are the tools used in his everyday life—such as a vehicle, home, bankroll, and clothes, etc.

Stereotypes, Opinions, and Myths

This section of the pimp scenario will cover all that's been heard about a pimp and the game in general. People tend to form an opinion to their own satisfaction, run their mouth on a myth, or just stay caught up in the hype of bullshit. Here is a list of twenty-one questions and twenty-one answers.

1. Is it true that a pimp would pimp anything, including female family members, or even a man?

2. What made you want to become a pimp?

3. Can you teach me the pimp game?

4. How do you get girls to sell their bodies for you?

5. Do you split, or let your hoes keep any money?

6. What are the most girls you ever had at once?

7. Do you have sex with your hoes?

8. How much do your hoes make?

9. Are you ever going to do something else besides pimp?

10. Do you bail your hoes out of jail?

11. Do you ever hit your girls?

12. Is it true that a pimp will sell his ass if he has no hoes?

13. How much do your hoes charge?

14. If they did all the work, why give you the money?

15. What do you do if another pimp gets one of your hoes?

16. How would you feel if a daughter of yours became a prostitute?

17. Where are your hoes?

18. How do you protect your girls?

19. Have you ever caught one of your girls stashing money?

20. Besides pimping, do you do something else on the side to make money?

21. Where do you pimp?

1. Is it true that a pimp will pimp anything, including female family
    members, or even a man?

As far as a pimp and female family members working for him as a
prostitute, it does occur on a circumstantial basis. A pimp isn't one who is
known to put up an objection to a woman's desire to become a prostitute,
or carry out a career as one. Therefore, if he was to find out that a woman
who is related to him decides to be a prostitute, chances are he would rather
see himself gaining the financial benefits, instead of someone else.

As far as a pimp going out of his way to turn out a female family member
to become a prostitute, in a situation where she isn't familiar with that
particular life, that isn't an unusual occurrence. But if a pimp finds out that
a daughter, or niece, or whatever female related to him is prostituting, he
will hold no discrimination toward receiving money from them.

When a lot of people ask that question, they are trying to see a pimp as
something less than themselves, as far as morality. But a pimp knows how
to accept the bitter with the sweet, and accept reality for what it is, while
another kind of individual involved in a matter like that would have no
idea how to respond or function.

The raw realities of many inner cities around the country have parents
and their children (grown ones) sharing a crack pipe together, getting high.
However, activity such as this may be a bit more common in a general ghetto,
or hood environment; therefore, it isn't going to be questioned the way
a person questions a pimp about the possibility of the conduct regarding
female family members being pimped. The unknown is what catches a
person's curiosity and can easily be interpreted as immoral, as opposed to
something that is more common and overlooked, such as parents getting
high with their kids.

For the matter of a pimp having homosexuals working in his stable as
drag queens, that is not a pimp—that is a homosexual himself. His home
is a homeful of dicks! There is no pussy running around his house. He
will not, under any circumstances, be acknowledged as a pimp by anyone
who knows better.

For those who indulge, they obviously don't discriminate who they'll
accept money from. It wouldn't be a surprise if they would pimp an animal
if they knew there were clients who indulge in bestiality. They are in a
category of their own, and they are not classified as a pimp.

Their conduct should not be misunderstood as a guideline in the rules
of pimping and hoeing!

2. What made you want to become a pimp?

People become pimps for several different reasons. You got some guys who grew up in a neighborhood where pimping and prostitution activity was always around them. They may have been doing one thing or the other to hustle, then jumped on the opportunity to see what it was like to have girls work for him as prostitutes.

Then when he gave it a try, it may have worked out better for him than what he was used to doing to get money. So he decided to push forward with a career as a pimp. Everybody's luck isn't the same in the beginning. Some guys experienced giving the game a try, and the first girl that jumps in a trick's car on his basis happens to split on him and fall short of the expectation—which was to turn a trick, get the money, and bring it back to him.

Since the first impression means a lot, those particular circumstances can cause a guy to lose interest in the pimp game and not have the confidence in himself to ever become successful. Now those who go through that in the beginning are usually schooled by seasoned pimps, who will tell them stories of their own, of how they've been through the same thing several times, and that there aren't very many pimps who hasn't. The topic of their reassurance is, "You got to stay down, to come up."

So some guys do the dipping and dabbing thing, while all along reflecting on their mistakes with each previous hoe, as they continue to pursue. After plenty of self-evaluating, he eventually develops a science of his own, which makes him capable of getting a longer run out of a prostitute and accumulating other girls to work in his stable while he's getting the same longevity and financial results from each one.

Another case in which guys become pimps is when a seasoned hoe turned them on to the game. In many situations like that, the guy may not have had any pimpin' in him at all. If he were to fall off the Empire State Building and shatter into a thousand pieces, there wouldn't be a pimp bone found in his body. The seasoned hoe that runs across this type of guy is usually one who has had a recent experience with a pimp and his stable, but for some reason or the other, she is no longer with him. So while she's renegading and freelancing, there's things going through her head, which will cause her to miss having a man to give her an impulsive motivation and bring her money to.

So what a hoe like this does is go out and come across some kind of "boyfriend" figure type of guy then give the news to him of how "she sells pussy for money. But if he'll be her man under those circumstances, the money that'll be made will be for the both of them." If the dude that she's trying to developed this bond with doesn't have too much going for himself, more than likely he'll take her up on the offer.

Besides free money, plus free pussy, how else can he look at it? All along, while this renegade, seasoned hoe is giving him this invitation, all she is really trying to do with her disoriented thoughts is turn this guy into the kind of pimp that she would rather have, as opposed to her previous one who was probably seasoned himself. All she is trying to do is take advantage of the young man's vulnerability to the game, and find or install the characteristics that she wishes she could have found in the pimp she was formerly with. But at the same time, do what she feels her hand originally calls for—hoe in!

She may have been jealous of other girls in her former pimp's stable, or felt she wasn't receiving the attention she deserved or desired. Or for whatever reasons. So now, here is this punk bitch, trying to stroke some "green" nigga's ego that he can get somewhere by her being his first hoe. Unfortunately for him, the relationship on that basis will not last longer than seven days, for one simple reason—the pimpin' always wins. And sooner before later, this hoe will think to herself, "Who am I trying to fool?" and go back to a program that she feels is more appropriate for her—a real pimp!

But for the short period of time that homeboy had encountered with this discombobulated little bitch, a seed was planted in him as far as pimping. And if he chooses to water and fertilize that seed within himself, he can very much so become a pimp.

Another reason why guys become pimps is they may have a friend from out of the neighborhood they grew up with who happens to be a pimp. And with curiosity kicking him in the ass, he ends up rolling with his pimp buddy and getting familiar with the pimp game by seeing his friend in action and observing everything that's going on, on the track. With some fellas, they're infatuated at first sight. They look and see how their friend is having hundreds, fifties, and twenties placed into his hand every couple of hours by, let's say, two or three girls throughout the night.

All that is going through this guy's head while he's observing the source of his pimp buddy's income is comparison to his own, regardless of what his hustle is. The next thing you know, he's weighing out all his options of which female he knows that will get down for him the way his pimp friend has girls getting down for him.

Usually when this burst of excitement crosses one's mind, just about any bitch can meet the criteria to be a candidate for him. From his girlfriend to baby's mother, or a young cute promiscuous girl from around his way that all his homies be fucking. Or if he's determined enough, the crack-cocaine-using hoe that hasn't lost her appeal yet.

Another example of what leads up to a person becoming a pimp is the inheritance of it. In some situations, there may be a young man who grew up in a household where he had always known his father to be an active pimp, and his mother to be a prostitute, whether active or inactive. Since this was all he knew while he was growing up, he feels comfortable with the lifestyle and sees himself being another generation of what is passed down in his family. There are several other reasons why guys become pimps, but these are just a few examples of some of the most common reasons.

3.   Can you teach me the pimp game?

Most people who ask this are about as serious as the question sounds. They're just making conversation. If one is honestly concerned, the pimp that is asked the question will be able to tell if his request is genuine or not, then take it from there.

The pimp game is not something that can just be taught. The concept can be explained, but the person would have to develop his own strategy. It's just like chess. A person can show you how each piece is supposed to be moved, and what the object of the game is. But it would be left up to you to come up with a strategy that works in order for you to win.

4. How do you get girls to sell their bodies for you?

Wouldn't the world like to know that one! I'm going to briefly go into the answer to that, but all that I would have to tell you is what anyone with good common sense would be able to come up with on his or her own.

First of all, any person whose self-esteem isn't really that high is missing something in life. And as far as a prostitute, she's missing companionship with a man that she's actually compatible with. Everybody needs love and companionship. A friend in their mate. Who else besides a pimp can a whore find this in? Let's take your everyday average trick for example.

Here's a guy who is a regular client for a prostitute. He and she are familiar with one another, by her meeting him on the basis of her line of duty. As time goes on, she may be considering him a nice person and thinking about taking him up on one of his many "Caption Save a Hoe" offers when times get hard for her. Besides, he, along with every other trick the hoe has ran across, has offered the hoe everything they think the hoe might be interested in. Regardless of how their offer is presented, it all boils down to them wanting that hoe to be a housewife.

Well, since a lot of hoes can't think any further than one hour at a time, they follow that instinct as soon as it comes to mind. So let's say now, she done moved herself, along with all of her property into the dude's house. He's so happy to have some inhouse pussy that he done forgot that she was a prostitute when he met her. She assures him and blows smoke up his ass that she actually hates that lifestyle, and she was only doing that because she had to support herself, and tells him how hard life is without a guy like him. And a whole lot of other Academy Award-winning scripts that she's laying out to him.

Well, even though his ignorance won't allow him to see it right away, the hoe, on the other hand, sees him for the trick he is. She'll never be able to become happy or be emotionally attached to a man who paid for her womanhood, just 'cause she had a For Sale sign on her ass. She might try to psych herself out for a minute and tell herself that there's a slight possibility that dude might become something she looks for in a man to an extent, but it'll never happen.

Any trick that accepts a prostitute off the streets into his home in hopes of developing a relationship with her has several insecurities about himself—regardless of what he has as far as materialistic things. If he was all that great of a person he presents himself to be to get one hooker, or the other to accept his invitation, then he should already have a wife or be in a steady relationship, to where he wouldn't take any type of interest in a hooker.

But due to him being desperate (like most tricks), she'll always have a lack of respect for him, and there will not be a moment out of the day where she can set her act to the side in his presence. He will only know her for the characteristics that she portrays in front of him.

Being sexually faithful to him is totally out of the question. 'Cause what he doesn't want to give her, she'll go out and do what she knows—to get what she wants. Once there's conflict and confusion in that household, and she's called all kinds of "dirty bitches" and "whores," and the guy is being told things like, "I was doing this shit before I met you! You knew what kind of woman I was before you begged me to come and live with you."

When all that silly shit starts happening, it's a wrap. A done deal. She'll leave just like she came, and be right back to square one. A pimp, on the other hand, is the most compatible male figure that can be in a hoe's life. He's the only type of man that she can meet and see right away that he is not in search of a woman for sexual gratification. This automatically causes her to have a sense of respect for him. He presents himself on a business level and probably the only kind of man on earth that can give a hoe some guidance to get something productive out of what she already accepts herself for doing.

Students go with teachers, patients go with doctors, and hoes go with pimps! A pimp is there to give a hoe emotional management, counseling, psychological therapy, financial assistance, and security. He is the one whom she has no problem submitting all of her honesty to. And if not anybody else, she respects him and depends on him as a young girl does her father. That's why hoes are accustomed to calling their pimps "daddy." So there it is there. The woman is not technically selling her body for him or herself; she's doing it for a purpose—a cause.

5.   Do you split, or let your hoes keep any money?

Absolutely not! That would be transgressing against a pimp's whole purpose as an agent for a prostitute. Once she's in the habit of breaking herself, she becomes accustomed to him being the one to handle all the financial matters.

There is no percentage being split, or money being distributed upon the understanding between a pimp and a prostitute. If she were to depend on self-reliability—whether it's managing her own money or dealing with her own responsibilities—she wouldn't have ever needed a pimp. All the areas she was weak in, as far as managing money, it's on the pimp to take care of all that.

All she has to do is go out and get it, and come back with it, and leave the rest to the man in charge. As long as her maintenance is being well kept, and she's in need for nothing—knowing that her earnings from her services as a prostitute is keeping all this covered, unlike before—then she's more than happy to see her pimp enjoy himself with the remainder of the money by doing whatever he wants to do with it.

6. What's the most girls you ever had at once?

This not-too-important question (unless your in a discussion with another pimp) is only answered if a pimp chooses not to be rude for a reaction to somebody being nosy.

A question like that is just like asking a drug dealer, "What is the most amount of his product he's ever had all at one time." Once again, those are one of those "make conversation" questions.

7. Do you have sex with your hoes?

Generally, it is not a good first impression on the pimp's behalf, because it is an unhealthy conduct, particularly in regards to confusing the woman who works for him. When a pimp and a prostitute settle in between each other, the two of them having sex with each other is not mentioned anywhere on the verbal contract.

Pimps who are young or either new to the game are the ones who are more expected not to be able to control their dick. Such misconduct causes a hoe to feel as if she is being conned out of her pussy and her financial benefits as a working prostitute on her pimp's basis. To simplify the matter, she'll feel as if she's spoiling the guy she works for.

She can also use his personal desire for sex as a weakness, and play on him with that in hopes of an advantage. If, or when, a sexual relationship does develop between a pimp and his hoe, in addition to their financial relationship, it usually happens at a time where both of them feel on a mutual basis that it will not affect their everyday conduct, as far as pimping and hoeing.

In many situations, it is very necessary for a pimp to allow this development to occur. A woman who has been putting in work for him, with every intent to make a rich man poor and a poor man rich on a daily basis, will feel as though he owes it to her to indulge with her in intimacy. Besides, tricks and clients can't satisfy her!

8.   How much do your hoes make?

The answer to this question coincides with the answer to question number 6.

9.   Are you ever going to do something else besides pimp?

People who ask that question are usually the ones that are curious to know if a pimp feels like his game has superiority over any other occupation. They're wondering if he really pimps because that's all he knows, or if he had a chance to do something else, would he?

What they don't know is that most pimps have already indulged in different occupations. The decision to become a pimp was a final alternative. If a pimp decides not to pimp anymore, he would more than likely resort to an occupation that is not illegal. There aren't many pimps that would see any sense in going back to an illegal occupation after they have been a pimp for a long period of time.

Just like most other "tax-free" occupations, anyone with good sense wouldn't turn their unlawfully earned money into something legal, to avoid a tax evasion.

10. Do you bail your hoes out of jail?

Depending on the circumstances will determine whether or not a pimp wants to bail his hoe out of jail. Hoes that get arrested all individually have a different situation with the law, as far as her arrest history.

If a hoe is bona fide, and she's with a reputable pimp who's financially set, more than likely her pimp will see to it that she is bailed out of jail ASAP every time, regardless of what her bail is. Being a bona fide hoe, it would be apparent that the amount of money that was put up for her bail would be made right back, and some!

Now, if a pimp has a hoe that gets arrested for her first prostitution case, but she has a clean criminal record, there would be no need to bail her out. It would be a waste of money. She'll still get out of jail with a citation to make a court appearance, in the same amount of time as if she were to get bailed out. But over all, it is a standard expectation for a pimp to be able to bail his hoes out when necessary.

11. Do you ever hit your girls?

For the most part, it often happens. Usually in the same concept of a man hitting his wife, or a parent spanking their child. When it occurs, it happens for diplomacy reasons. The only difference is, when a pimp does it, it stands out more in the negative aspect. People who misunderstand pimps and don't bother to see them in any other way than a pessimistic point of view tend to use any negativity against them in an effort to badger their character.

Pimps use their gift of counseling after the discipline of one of their employees, so the hoe can understand the logic of what led up to violence being a necessity. Some women have a fetish to be abused, and they won't respect their pimp as an authority figure if he doesn't hit her. These type of hoes are bad luck in a pimp's program. To maintain them, a pimp has to find himself coming out of character from time to time just to communicate with them.

This will cause other hoes in the stable to analyze the pimp's tolerance, and then they'll throw something in his face that they observed (for an excuse) with him, and the hoe that desires negative attention.

If this type of hoe is the only girl that the pimp has at the time, then that type of malfunction can be worked out. But if she's one out of a stable of other hoes, she will eventually become a problem and will not last. A pimp would preferably deal with hoes that he doesn't have to ever put his hands on. That way, he would be living up to his image as a gentleman—unlike the husband who is always the aggressor in an abusive relationship with his wife—because he doesn't know how to manage his emotions.

Or like an abusive parent who hits their children beyond what's necessary, due to their personal problems, a pimp would rather refrain from any dysfunctional activity that has any similarities with, or resemblance to, what his persona opposes to.

12. Is it true that a pimp will sell his ass if he has no hoes?

No, it is not true! Different people have different motives that lead up to them having the nerve to ask this stupid-ass question. The majority of people who would ask that question are the ones who are in the subconscious denial of the existence of pimps. In more simplified terms—they don't like pimps! For whatever reason. That question is not asked out of people wondering if the myth is true or not, 'cause no one believes in their hearts that it's true while they're asking it.

Instead, they'll ask that question to see what kind of reaction they'll get. A lot of people envy pimps, and are jealous of them. So what they do in an effort to balance out whatever insecurities they may feel while a pimp is in their presence is ask such question in an effort to degrade a pimp. Since their intentions are to get into a debate with the pimp and have him at their mercy of the conversation, while all along they'll try to see how far they can go, there is no simple answer to put that question to a halt.

For example, a person might say, "Hey, man, I heard that a 'real pimp' will sell his own ass if he doesn't have a hoe working for him. Is that true?" And then the pimp tells him in response to his question, "Of course not." Then the usual response to that answer will be, "Then you isn't no real pimp."

So basically, the person who brought the matter up just put the pimp in a "catch 22." Either the pimp falsely admits to being a potential homosexual, or he won't be considered a real pimp—at least not by the person who asked the question. (Like his opinion matters.) A more appropriate answer to a question like that would be one that's just as disrespectful as the question itself: "No, I wouldn't sell my own ass if I didn't have any hoes. I would slap a wig and some heels on you, and make you sell your ass for me."

Now, a response like that would make the average guy want to fight. But if he does anything else besides throw a blow and decides to keep it at a social level—hostile or calm—it will be brought to his attention that he brought that on himself. When people put out negative energy, that's what usually comes back to them. Besides, the people who ask questions like that are only aiming for the conversation to lead to the pimp justifying for himself not to be a potential homosexual, so they can get a personal amusement out of a pimp taking them seriously enough to explain themselves to.

So the best way to respond to a question like that is with the same negative energy that the question brought. The reality of the "mythical" matter is, of course, a pimp wouldn't walk in the shoes of a prostitute if he temporarily didn't have a hoe working for him. Allow me to present the logic of the whole matter to you.

First of all, a homosexual can be found in many different people from all different kinds of lifestyles, occupations, and hustles. There can be a person who is known as an active gang member from a reputable street gang. Let's say for one reason or another, this person becomes a homosexual to whatever extent, and everyone that matters becomes aware of this. What would happen, as far as his fellow gang associates are concerned (since they all represent the same thing), is they would more than likely hurt this guy, cut his tattoos of their gang off of his body (if he has any), and tell him to keep their gang out of his mouth. That would be at the least.

At the most, they would kill him. The point is, he's a disgrace to himself, and his former homies are not going to give him an opportunity to be a disgrace to them by being a homosexual while he's a representative of their gang. It's not going down!

Over all, does that put a black eye in the world of gangbanging? Of course it doesn't. Here's another example: There are homosexuals who sell drugs. That's right. there are some who are certified drug dealers. Question is, does their own personal sexual preference have an effect on the general reputation of drug dealers? Not that I ever heard of.

Why hasn't anyone put together a myth that states something about a drug dealer being a potential homosexual? A person who's familiar with the hood has seen, or is aware of, a gay drug dealer. But who can honestly say that they're aware of, or seen, a gay pimp? Nobody!

They may try to exaggerate a bullshit scenario to make as if they have some applicable information, but they are only trying to convince themselves more than anyone else. People who don't like pimps go out of the way to take a myth and run with it without any logics to back it up.

Are people envious at the thought of gangbangers? No! How about drug dealers? Not usually! If someone is jealous of a drug dealer, it's usually on a personal basis with a particular drug dealer—but not the gang as a whole.

Here are some of the things that a pimp would resort to according to his status, if he doesn't have a hoe. A successful pimp won't be long without a hoe, 'cause if he's already financially comfortable and has game as far as acknowledgment with several hoes, especially ones that had worked for him before. His name as a pimp will campaign for itself. He doesn't have to resort to an emergency financial plan. He'll have him some more hoes before anyone even realizes that he was down to a zero count in his stable.

As far as the pimps who are just starting to pick up the pace, if one of them don't have a hoe, he'll be well taken care of by his pimp partners financially (that's if his pockets aren't already all right) until he comes up with a hoe. (Which should be his main goal at all times anyway.) Successful or fortunate pimps will not leave a persistent pimp hanging during the time of a temporary setback.

Then you got the same kind of young pimps who have too much pride to ask anybody for anything. A person of this nature usually dips and dabs into his previous hustle, until he finally gets a hoe on a stable basis. Then he'll go full-fledge with his pimping. Then there are those that will resort in criminal activity to get money to hold him down until he gets a hoe. Then there are those who have always had a separate source of income aside from pimping. For example, the owner or manager of a small business. So, with or without a hoe, money is never an issue for him. So the myth about a pimp selling his own ass is total nonsense. People like to say, along with making that comment, that they "read it out of a book." Bullshit! They picked up on that myth from someone else they heard talking out of their ass. Then they felt that they had a perfect opportunity to hit somebody with that when they're talking to a pimp themselves.

13. How much do your hoes charge?

In some situations, this is another one of those questions that are used to either make conversation, or for the person who's asking it, to see if they can start a series of questions. But not in all situations. Sometimes, depending on who the person is, it is a legitimate question to ask 'cause the person may actually be considering turning a date with one of the girls, and would only like to see if the prices are affordable for him.

This type of person would more than likely be someone who works at a job somewhere in the vicinity of the pimp's everyday whereabouts, and has an "okay" rapport with him. How the pimp chooses to carry on the financial matter with the guy is totally up to him. He may knock the price up a notch or two in an effort to accumulate a high-paying client for his girls.

Or he may be the kind of pimp who feels it isn't his position to carry on these types of discussions with a potential john, and would rather cut the conversation short and give the guy the hoe's cell phone number so he can get in touch with her himself and take it from there. A total stranger, especially one who's hanging around an area where there are pimps and prostitutes, has zero chance of getting that question answered. In an environment like that, a trick or a potential john would be expected to approach a woman herself, and ask her all that. There's no need for him to be shy. Besides, the women are out there selling pussy. So anyone who's a stranger and has the nerve to approach a pimp on that basis is more than likely an undercover police officer who has the intent to arrest a pimp for the act of procuring.

14. If they did all the work, why give you the money?

The answer to this question coincides with the answers to questions number 4 and 5.

15) What do you do if another pimp gets one of your hoes?

When people ask this question, they have the general scenario in their mind of how a man would usually react to losing his woman to another man. There's a big difference! For a regular guy in a relationship with a woman, it is not within her expectations to commit the acts of fornication or adultery. Let alone, all out leaving her man for another one.

That act would be considered coldhearted in most people's eyes. If there's someone who hasn't actually lived through that experience, they've at least seen it on television shows: "I've brought you here today to let you know that I've been seeing somebody else, and I don't want to be with you anymore," the woman will say to her just dismissed spouse.

Then as soon as the other guy comes out, the fella who just received the bad news attacks the other guy, and the fight is on. The person who is really at fault in the matter (which happens to be the woman) is standing on the sideline, watching the brawl between the two guys, trying to remain as guilt free as possible. The guy who was originally with her did not manage his emotions correctly, and he takes the whole matter out on the other guy. He is subconsciously in denial of his woman actually being the one responsible of making the decision of wanting to be with somebody else. He doesn't want to accept the fact that it was her choice to become involved with another man. But the reality of the situation is what it is!

She used her God-given advantage of being a woman—who has the choice of who she wants to be with—and she chose to be with somebody else. Reality usually sets in on the guy who comes out on the raw end of this scenario, but sometimes it takes a while.

Now here's how it works with a pimp, and the women they deal with. First of all, a pimp sees a woman he initiates as his working prostitute "going" as soon as she "comes." It is within her expectations to leave unexpectedly. And when they do leave, they are free of guilt. They'll tell themselves that their previous pimp really didn't care about them no way; otherwise, he wouldn't have had them working the streets and selling their bodies.

That's usually one of the thoughts that cross their mind when they're in their "guilt-free" mode, after they done left their pimp for some square type of dude—a sugar daddy or a boyfriend figure. However, that wasn't the case when she was with her pimp. As far as a hoe leaving her previous pimp for another one, that is a common occurrence in the game.

There are rules and standards along with "codes" to go by in the pimp game. The actions and performances of a hoe that's up under a pimp is a reflection of the instructions he gives her to abide by while she's in the line of her duty out on the hoe stroll. The precautionary instructions that a pimp enforces on his hoes is to prevent the risk of losing her to another pimp. Some of the main rules laid out on the table to the hoe during her orientation process is to "not" acknowledge another pimp visually, verbally, or physically!

And they're also told that the best way to avoid the possibility of any of that occurring is to not even allow another pimp to come within their space where they're close enough for that kind of activity to be possible. Some hoes that work for pimps develop the instinct to see heavy pimp activity heading in their direction from a distance, and start maneuvering their way around it before it reaches them.

In many situations, it is not up to the hoe how hard she gets sweated by a pimp. A lot of pimps are very crafty, persistent, and aggressive when it comes to trying to knock another pimp for his hoe, or just trying to accumulate some "fresh work." A hoe that shows signs of weakness while she's working the track for another pimp, by doing things like "smiling," not putting forth very much effort to get away from a pimp's verbal approach (whether he's on foot or driving by), is more than likely to get sweated the hardest by a seasoned pimp. 'Cause those type of reactions from her reflect on *her* pimp and the instructions he gave her. So the seasoned pimp is going to pick up the impression that she's under someone who is along the lines of an amateur, or the hoe is just a defiant little bitch who likes anything that's in front of her at the moment.

Now a hoe that is loyal to her pimp and their agreed agenda doesn't find herself in situations like that. But for the loose one's that do find themselves in those types of situations, they're more than likely to get knocked.

Some hoes that go from pimp to pimp on a constant basis are what are considered "Choosie Suzie" hoes. A pimp who knows this type of hoe's reputation works her as much as possible and gets as much out of her as he can while he has her before she "blows up" (runs off) and ends up with another pimp.

These types of hoes do not affect a pimp's reputation, as far as being able to maintain a hoe for a long period of time. And they do not cause any conflict or tension between pimps, when one who just had her is served the news that she's now with whoever else. It was expected of her. Hoes like that are free from all emotion, and are fascinated with seeing what a different pimp's program is like.

That's just the matter with the Choosie Suzies. A hoe is like the weather; they'll change their mind, at any time! There are several different reasons why they leave their pimps in the blink of an eye. And every time it's done, they have a reason or an excuse that's good enough for themselves to remain free of guilt. They'll think things to themselves like, "Oh, he's a pimp. He'll be able to get another girl." And many other things along those lines. She'll reflect on the things she's been through with her former pimp, and focus in on what can be generally described as negativity.

It might be things like physical discipline, or something that affected her emotionally. Or maybe even the standards of her former pimp's management skills. Regardless of what it could have been, or how many different things it could be, he's the bad guy! The same thing that she accepted him and loved him for when she was with him will be the same things that she projects in her mind to perceive him as a monster. And the funny thing about it is she'll accept those things from the next pimp she's with—until she's no longer with him.

Even though a hoe may not ever realize it, these types of series in her life will become repetitive, as long as she remains the kind of person she is. The thing about a pimp is he already knows this. It's common knowledge to him. He sees all of this in a hoe the very second she accepts his invitation to work for him as a prostitute. That's why when he loses a hoe in the name of the game, there are no hard feelings. Don't get me wrong, every situation isn't the same, and you do have some pimps that become emotionally attached to their hoes. Not necessarily on some lovey-dovey shit, but rather the love of her performance she put in for him.

Those rare situations may cause a pimp to have a reaction to getting knocked for his hoe, which would be similar to how a regular guy may react to getting knocked for his girlfriend or wife. But that is not on a usual basis. Most pimps look at it like this: the bitch wasn't a virgin when they met her. The same way that she feels that you're the one who's worth her giving her all to, is the same way that she felt about somebody before you. A current pimp of hers won't be her last, if not her first. Pimps try to make sure that they refrain from falling out with another man over this type of woman, 'cause they know that once there's beef with another man, he and the other guy can be enemies for life. But that same bitch that was the root of that beef will not belong to neither one of them for life. She'll have moved on in life, and these two guys will still be enemies.

16. How would you feel if a daughter of yours became a prostitute?

Now this question amongst the many of them would be considered the fairest one to ask, depending on who's asking it. Unfortunately, the person who would have the nerve to ask it quicker than anybody else would be a hypocrite. You know, the type of guy who sells drugs, and has got his dick sucked in exchange for some of his product, from a young attractive girl who gets high, and, most important of all, happens to be someone's daughter!

Or the type of guy who, at one point or another in his life, has ran a train (one girl with multiple sex partners, all in one episode) on a girl with his friends. As soon as this kind of dude asks a pimp a question about how he would feel if his daughter ended up becoming like one of the girls that work for him, then the pimp reminds him of the activities that he's indulged in, that doesn't make him any better than a pimp, as far as what's been done to "someone's daughter." Automatically the guy who asked the question gets into the state of denial.

"Oh, as a matter of fact, I ain't ever been one to get down like that homie! I only mentioned it because I got a daughter of my own"—and all that other bullshit he'll say.

When that kind if person asks that question, there's no easy conclusion to come to that'll put an end to it. The question was asked, just like some of the others, with the intent to start conflict and argument. The guy asking the question didn't take no regard for his mother, daughter, sister, and/or spouse when he committed the acts he did with whoever and however many girls. So therefore, he's not entitled to the real answer.

An appropriate answer to a question like that, for somebody who has an actual concern and isn't trying to badger a pimp's image is this: If a pimp has a daughter who grows up and becomes a prostitute in particular—out of all of the many other things that a parent wouldn't be proud of—believe it or not, he would probably accept it, and I'll tell you why. For the most part, he'll have to recall to himself how many different girls through his career would probably not have become a prostitute if they've never met him.

In addition to that, his daughter, being one who grew up around the game and not being a stranger to it from day one, would not be vulnerable or easily tricked or finessed into becoming a prostitute by some intelligent source of pimpin'. Anything that some slick nigga could say to her is more than likely something she's heard her father say to girls in the house on several different occasions growing up. Therefore, if her father were to become aware of her making a decision to sell her pussy, he wouldn't let his emotions get involved and remain levelheaded about the whole matter.

Why? 'Cause he knows that the knowledge of the game that she inherited from being in a household with that activity going on, whatever her reason was for making that decision, she's sure of it; and there's no talking that can be done that will change anything. Besides, how many children grew up and met the expectations their parents set for them?

17. Where's your hoes at?

The most appropriate response to this question would be to all out ignore the person who asked it, in the rudest form imaginable. Why? 'Cause that question has a deeper meaning than what the words project. A more relevant interpretation of that question is, "Prove to me you're a pimp. I doubt you. Prove yourself."

There are only a few who would ask this question that are an exception to that interpretation. For example, if a young girl (within reasonable age) recognizes a guy as a pimp, and she asks that question, there's a possibility that she's fascinated by him, and may even be considering seeing what his program is like. All she wouldn't mind seeing is a couple of girls who contribute to who he proclaims to be. To see if she can analyze them and see if they're happy with catering to a pimp.

Besides that, and other scenarios similar to that, people will ask that question almost off of an instinct to start a series of questions, while they're in that denial frame of mind. (In which I described more than once.) I mean really, listen to the question, "Where's your hoes at?"

Can one really expect for a pimp to have his hoes present every moment of his existence! Maybe a dumb ass would think that. But what they're really getting at is convincing themselves that the person claiming to be a pimp may not be one after all. And if he does anything but produce his hoes right there at their request, they'll have more of a reason to cater to their own doubt. There isn't really any productive conversation that will come out of a question like that.

18. How do you protect your girls?

It makes sense for someone to wonder what kind of source of security a pimp has for the women who work for him. As it already goes without saying, a pimp gives a woman that works for him guidance and precautionary instructions on how to deal with any and all of the dangers that she may encounter in her line of duty.

How the woman chooses to abide by those rules will determine the outcome of any unexpected situation. There's an old phrase that sport coaches have always used to encourage their teams: "If you stay ready, you ain't gotta get ready." Well, as far as a pimp and his position being similar to coaches, he should already be mentally equipped with the precautionary instructions that apply to his particular program for his hoes.

We'll use the most common form of prostitution as an example—streetwalkers. These girls must receive a thorough rundown of all the possibilities of the possible occurrences while they're working the streets. Such as how to screen a trick or potential john for any unordinary vibes that she can find. Also how to go about determining if the person approaching her is really an undercover cop, or not. Tricks that indulge in sex with girls, and then demand for the money back.

Tricks who won't let them out of the car upon their request. Other pimps trying to approach them in an effort to recruit. Other hoes who are natives of that neighborhood trying to enforce territorial standards on them. Gang members and/or drug dealers who may try to persuade them into a state of distraction, for their own benefits. Other hoes that work for their pimp try to trick one's hoe into being led off somewhere the foreign source of pimpin' is at. (Another trickery method used in an effort to recruit.) Running across lesbians, who already have a vendetta toward men, and would just love to take a bite out of a pimp's empire. Besides, lesbians already think that if a woman allows herself to be with a pimp, she'll be easy game for a lesbian to turn her attention away from the pimp, and on to her ideas of exploitation.

And last but definitely not least, the religious people. The ones who underestimate the strong will of a prostitute, and continuously sweat them while they use their technique of guilt trip that they'll try to put on the prostitute by mentioning religion and how it opposes to prostitution. Also, they mention the possibility of "You can die in your life of sin and never have a chance to repent"—and all that good shit. But those religious people go home and drink their alcohol, and indulge in premarital sex with their spouse, and not even allow the possibility of dying in their own sinful ways cross their mind.

The best source of security that a pimp can provide his woman is making her aware of all these possible encounters, and the best way to go about them when they occur. Besides, he cannot hold her hand to literally guide her in her line of duty. Within the first two weeks of a hoe working for a particular pimp, she will experience a large portion of the mentioned possibilities. Depending on the outcome of whichever one of them a woman may go through, due to her pimp's instructions, will cause her to determine if he is the appropriate man for her to depend on for guidance.

19. Have you ever caught one of your hoes stashing money?

When people ask this question, they see a hoe being one who deceives men so much, to where they couldn't imagine a pimp being an exception. It is not a usual occurrence for one, if the pimp's managing skills are up to par. Anything that the hoe would be expecting to receive would automatically happen without her deceiving her pimp, by not giving him all the money.

Besides, what would the hoe have to show for in merchandise in front of her pimp that wouldn't be a dead giveaway? Unless it was a gift from one of the hoe's clients. Anything that she produces would make it obvious that it was done with some money that the pimp knew nothing about. Now that usually doesn't happen 'cause the hoe isn't that stupid, and neither is the pimp.

However, there are two exceptional circumstances. The first one is, if the hoe is a drug addict. If this caliber of a hoe feels to any extent that her man's management skills fall short—as far as how high she wants to get—and she knows where a nearby drug connection is at that she can go straight to, to get her issue, instead of depending on pimpin' every single time. You better believe that she's going to be having it her way with some money that her pimp will never know about.

And the second exception is this: If there is a woman with her pimp, and she's making evacuation plans to leave him—whether for another pimp, or just to go on about her way—she's going to be financially prepared if her thought of leaving him was anticipated.

The purpose of stacking money on the low for the point of leaving her current pimp, for the next one, is to have an initiation fee.

As far as the ones who are leaving to go on about their way, she'll need money to get from point A to point B.

20. Besides pimping, do you do something else on the side to make money?

Sure! There's plenty of pimps who have a separate source of income. The matter of knowing which pimp does or does not is about as much a mystery as "how far does the universe expand?"

You have pimps that are 100 percent pimps. Straight laced, no chase. They get it all from the womb (women) and none from the spoon (drugs). Then there are those who are just as much pimp at heart, classification, and performance, but something pertaining to them in their life is a reason they may have a separate source of income. I'm going to make some examples out of matters that are legal first.

Let's say here's a pimp on parole. One of his conditions is to maintain employment. He can't pimp from a jail cell; and as a man being in the business matters to other people's lives, he now has to depend on his own advice given to himself. There's not many options in the matter. So what does pimpin' do? It gets a job.

Yeah, he still has hoes working for him and contributing to his full-fledge life as a pimp. But he has a job. Let's say it's only four hours a day. Enough to keep parole from twisting his arm and threatening to violate him if he can't produce a good enough explanation of how he has the money to accumulate his wealth. His parole officer doesn't know he's pimping, and his hoes don't know he's working. Not like having a job is the biggest must-keep secret in the pimp game.

But there's a saying, which states, "Find out as much as possible about the hoe, and allow her to know very little about you." That particular formula is necessary in a matter like this. Since no hoe is promised to any pimp tomorrow. A hoe that knows too much of his business will take it out of the door with her. Hoes talk too much, pimps talk too much, people talk too much.

There is no exception to a person's capability of gossiping! So once a pimp's business is put into circulation like that, he'll be hearing it come back at him in ways that are not intended to be beneficial for him. He may even hear them from sources that have matters of their own. Only difference is they may have been a little more better at not letting their business get into circulation like his was.

Yeah, he may know that he has that four-hour-a-day job to avoid going back to prison, but who cares what the reason is. Something to gossip about is what it is. Anyone in his or her right frame of mind would rather be a free pimp, instead of an incarcerated one, where the career is practically on hold.

In other legal situations, there might be a pimp who owns or manages a small business just to maintain pay stubs to avoid a tax evasion, while all along his main source of income is really through his pimping. Owning or managing a business is not that big of a physical responsibility as someone might think. Hell, you even got pimps who receive county checks. Some pimps will keep a legal source of income on the side just in case the day comes where they don't have an active prostitute working for them. It won't affect them financially, and they'll be all right until they do come up on another hoe. Others do what they got to do legally until *they* feel comfortable enough to drop everything else, and go full-fledge with his pimping, with no looking back.

Now I'm going to go to the other side of the separate source of income matter—the illegal matters! With a lot of illegal alternatives, some of them come along with the game. While some of them even require the hoe's assistance. You got your pimps who teach their girls how to boost (shoplift), while some hoes already come equipped with that trade. It serves its purpose, as far as a pimp, his hoe and their source of income. So it's official.

Then there are prostitutes who are under a pimp that are really good at hitting a lick (robbery or rip off). Some hoes bring more money home after hitting one lick, than they would have from a month's earnings of "flat backing" (sex). Some hoes are built for that, while others just don't have it in them.

The ones who are skilled will leave from a trick's presence with more than just two or three twenty-dollar bills that he handed her for a blow job. By the time he realizes that his whole wallet is gone, along with his expensive watch, it's too late. He'll be halfway home, and the hoe will be all the way gone!

Now, those two scenarios I just used as examples are highly common and acceptable in the pimping and prostitution trade. Also, they won't get any critical feedback. Why? 'Cause the hoe is still doing all the work, while the pimp is orchestrating it.

Then you got what is probably the most common, and somewhat a critical, illegal alternative in the game—the "Sack-Mack." Yeah, he's a pimp. You can't take that from one who's already been classified. But he's risking taking a felony penitentiary chance, and the man is doing all the work. Not the woman. Besides, if a guy has a woman selling drugs for him under any other circumstances than being a couple outside of any regards to pimping and prostitution, then the dude will never be able to take full control of that woman. Pimps work best with hoes, not hustler bitches.

And if the guy is doing anything else but try to bring this "willing" female hustler to grounds of prostitution in his financial favor, then he is wasting his time. Since that is obvious—and goes without saying—a pimp is on his own during the moments of this alternative hustle. The good thing about any pimp that feels that the sack-mack alternative is necessary is he knows how much of a risk he's taking, and he should be more motivated during that obstacle than any other.

Due to the fact that drug dealing is a twenty-hour-a-day job (drug dealers get four hours of sleep each day), and pimping is a twenty-five-hour-a day job (pimps pimp in their sleep during that one extra hour), you cannot do both at the same time.

So the sack-mack alternative causes one to really get in hot pursuit of a new prostitute (not a substitute) before his ass goes down by the long arm of the law for a hustle that he doesn't even major in.

21. Where do you be pimping at?

I had to save the dumbest for last. This question, just like 6, 8, and 17 has absolutely no good motive behind it.

It is a waste of hot air that would be put to better use by inhaling a pull of some crack smoke! It's another one of those "let me see if I can get a pimp opened with a series of questions, starting with this one" kind of matters.

In this section of the stereotypes, opinions, and myths, I have covered the twenty-one most-asked questions that pimps have heard, or will hear. But everything that a person has to say about a pimp does not always come out in a questionable form. A lot of things that are said are usually stereotypical comments, which mostly come out in an ignorant manner and don't necessarily require feedback.

The person that said it feels good doing just that is trying to impress themselves. There are thousand of those comments, and they're not worth justifying for, due to their un-importance.

Assassinating an Image

Throughout the years, the movie industry and people who like to dwell on stereotypes have worked hand in hand. First, the stereotypes will be floating about in the communities, then somebody in the movie industry gets their hands on it, writes it in a script; then the next thing that happens, you're watching it on your television set. For those who call themselves being entertained by what the media projected to them, as far as the pimp is concerned, people of all different creeds, colors, lifestyles, and ages will piece together all they've seen and form their own opinion about a pimp.

Then by the time they run across a pimp in real life, they'll have some inaccurate form of opinion to voice—if the opportunity presents itself to them. Or they'll quote a line or scene from something that the media portrayed.

Look how the media projects pimps to the public eye. In the 1970s TV show *Starsky & Hutch*, there was a character by the name of Huggy Bear, who happened to be a pimp on the show. His role consisted of him being a snitch that was telling the two cops (Starsky and Hutch) whatever useful information he had, so he could carry out his program as a pimp.

Then that same character shows up years later in the Wayans brothers produced movie *I'm Gonna Git You, Sucker*, as Huggy Bear, walking down the street with glass platform shoes on with a goldfish inside of one.

As he's walking past crowds of people on the sidewalk, there are excessive cries of laughter coming from everybody he passes, due to his outdated demeanor and his ridiculed dress code. As a result of him being overwhelmed with a feeling of humiliation and embarrassment, he begins to run past those crowds of people. Then his shoe with the goldfish inside of it breaks, and the goldfish is flopping around on the ground.

All the way back to the days where the United States had its transitional phase in segregated matters, the white man had a vengeance for pimps. Reason being, as soon as blacks got their civil rights, the black man wasted no time indulging in interracial relationships with white women. Then at that particular time, the white man felt as though the black man was getting a little too out of hand by including white women in his stable of prostitutes. Especially in the major cities located in the northern hemisphere of the United States such as Milwaukee, Wisconsin; Detroit, Michigan; New York City, New York; Oakland, California; Chicago, Illinois; Portland, Oregon; and Seattle, Washington.

The next thing you know, it spread like wildfire. Pimps from all different sections of the United States had white women, amongst other ethnics, besides black, working for them as prostitutes. Immediately, law officials in several states came up with laws to make sure that pimping was an illegal act. The state of California's penal law for a pimp charge is 266h. Pimping. And 266i. Pandering. Both of those charges carry three, four, or six years state prison time. And if the girl was a minor under the age of sixteen, the sentence carries three, six, or eight years state prison.

The state of New York has a similar law in the same regard, which is called "Promoting Prostitution and Patronizing a Prostitute." Law officials everywhere had even came up with specific laws to break down any possible activity that a pimp could indulge in—in regards to his profession—and consider it an illegal act. Then to top it off, they even have a law out in those particular regard called "White Slavery." (What a coincidence.)

It wasn't until the white woman became involved with black pimps that those laws were enforced. The white man did not appreciate it. And not only did he want to enforce a law on the matter, he also wanted to crush the image of the black pimp. That's what his intentions are through the media. That's how characters like Huggy Bear came about.

Even the black-produced films of today do not even realize the subliminal message that they put out, as far as how the pimp should be perceived. They have been so caught up in the hype of pimps being something humorous, or comical, that they don't know any better when they have actors portray these roles.

Let's take the 2001 movie *How High* for example. In that movie, there was a pimp by the name of Baby Powder, and his assistant. Throughout the movie, the characteristics as a pimp that Baby Powder and his assistant were portraying was a little too over the top. Then toward the end of the movie, Baby Powder and his assistant get beat up, and their heads smashed through the windshield of their Cadillac by an Oriental trick, who was playing "Caption Save a Hoe" for the prostitutes. Then the prostitutes that work for Baby Powder grabbed the Oriental by the arm, and referred to Baby Powder as a "bitch."

In real life, incidents like that don't happen. In the 2003 Ice Cube film *Friday After Next*, there was a pimp character by the name of Money Mike. On several occasions throughout the movie, the pimp character was comical and did not give reason to any extent of why a pimp should be taken seriously. There was even one scene in the movie where the pimp character came close to getting sexually assaulted by another man.

These types of observations by the public are part of the stereotypes that come about. When people meet or comes across a pimp in real life, they find themselves asking him about something that they have seen in a movie like that. People will only register that type of false impression of the black pimp from fictitious movies 'cause the directors and screenwriters don't know any better. And it probably wouldn't make any difference if they did. They're going to give the people what they want, as long as it sells!

That's only the case of the fictitious half of the media. When the reality of pimping hits the public eye, in the fashion of the production company allowing real pimps to show the game for what it is, instead of actors, no one is able to recall anything that was funny, degrading, humiliating, humorous, sexually unbalanced, or demoralizing to one's self as a pimp.

There are highly known documentaries that HBO promoted and filmed such as, *Pimps Up, Hoes Down* and *Hookers on the Point*. Those two documentaries (amongst many smaller-produced ones) allowed America to take a sneak peek into the true world of pimps and prostitutes. The feedback that the world gives to those kinds of exposures is nothing like the silly feedback that is given in response to a fictitious movie. When a person hears the real from the real, it's respected. When a person sees it projected on the big screen out of somebody's imagination, it just doesn't come out right.

Another highly publicized documentary was the Hughes Brothers' *American Pimp*. In the documentary, which footage was taken in various places in the country, pimps were interviewed, and brief insight was given on the life of pimps and prostitutes.

In 1973, the Oakland, California-based movie *The Mack*, which starred Max Julian and Richard Prior, was the first and, to this day, the only major motion picture based on pimping. At the time of the making of the movie, real-life pimps had assisted in the writing of the script, so that way no one would have to include imagination or guessing to put together what pimps really go through.

With the exception of the change of style, fashion, and attire due to a gap in the era of the movie, up until recent day, the situations and occurrences that were shown in the movie are the same ones that occur in a lot of pimps' lives now. As far as going to prison. Dealing with crooked cops. Old acquaintances with drug dealers. Shootouts, murders, and drug addiction.

That movie was made in a replicated image of how certain things went on in the pimp game back in those days. There wasn't anything funny or comical about it then. And there sure isn't anything funny about it now. Times have only gotten harder for pimps, along with other members who indulge in illegal activities. Everything a pimp does now has to be done in a strategic manner 'cause minor slip-ups now cost a person's wealth, freedom, or life.

People carry on with misconceptions whether they're sure of what they're saying or not, just to have something to talk about. And a pimp has always been one to catch somebody's attention.

The Reality

A lot of different people, for their own reasons tend to let their imagination run wild at the thought of possibly becoming a pimp. They place an optimistic scene in their mind of themselves being surrounded by beautiful women of all different races, treating him like a king. He's driving the finest cars of his choice. Having sex and orgies with all of these women at his discretion. Wearing all the jewelry he's ever desired, and giving orders to women without any talkback from them.

Not only has he projected this image in his mind, in which he sees so clearly. He can also see the easy paths that he'll take to get there as well. He sees himself putting his gangster hand down, and robbing at least five different pimps for their hoes. Going to a known hoe stroll, and clearing it out by letting off rounds of his AK-47 assault rifle . . . followed by shots from his AR-15. Bang on his chest a couple of times, like King Kong or somebody else. Then shout out loud for everybody on the block to hear, "I run this mothafucka now! Can't no pimps, hoes, crackhead hoes, or anybody get money on this track without going through me first? Only my bitches can work this track, and whoever else that I allow. So I'm here to let you know that there's a new sheriff in town, and I'm running this shit, so don't get it twisted."

And he just has it his way from there on out. Well, unfortunately for that young fellow with the wild imagination, that image in his head will never get him any farther than having something to think about. Or something to share in partial with somebody that he's telling how he can become a pimp anytime he wants to.

What people tend to forget when they take some kind of interest in a matter is that there's a downside to every game to go along with the upside. There is just no one-way easy street—and that's it. Especially in the pimp game. On a daily basis, there are upsides and downsides that a pimp has to deal with constantly. Not so much 'cause of the obstacles that may get in his path, 'cause that goes without saying for anyone in an underworld lifestyle. But more for the fact that he's dealing with other human beings (his women), instead of a product.

Therefore, he has to always remain prepared to manage and have one of those "best thing to do in this situation" solutions at any given, unexpected moment of the day or night. Now if that's not what you call "taking the upside with the downside" on a day-in-day-out basis, then I don't know what it is. The longevity in the game, along with success on the financial basis, is all rewards for a pimp knowing how to master the art of dealing with other minds. These are the requirements that one should be capable of doing, in order to master that art.

Inspiring, motivating, assuring, therapeutic, ego boosting, counseling, and finessing. Those are the major tools that a pimp should be equipped with. A pimp without that is like a new car with no gas; a person will look good sitting in it, but it won't get them anywhere. What should be understood is that, it is not a difficult task to have a woman submit and sell her body upon a man's request. Especially if she really digs the guy. That's in the law of a woman doing whatever her man tells her to do. However, the qualifications of each man as an individual may differ in order for him to know what will work best for him if he chooses to pursue the career of a pimp. Harsh, but true—the more tools a pimp has, the better his catching game will be.

Think about it. Here's a guy with at least one updated model car. A two-bedroom apartment in a designated area, free from distractions. A more-than-impressive wardrobe. A healthy bankroll. With just that right there, he's taking the leadership role, and any woman that he brings to the presence of all this for reasons of interview and invitation will see him as a dependable source, due to his presentation.

In case there are no other hoes that he would be able to show for at that particular moment, and the young lady doesn't bite her tongue on wanting to know why, whatever one-lined quick answer that the gentleman comes up with will be accepted by this woman. Plain and simple, she will believe him for one reason: he has the materialistic to back up his self-proclaimed title!

During the acceptance of his invitation to be a part of everything he is and has, by simply giving an honest effort as his working prostitute, the man will also have to bring to the newly recruited girls' attention that, in his line of business, he has a goal to accumulate more women under the same circumstances. Then go on farther to explain to her the specifics so she will understand the logic of his wishes, and the necessity of his desire to have as many women as possible working for him.

Now under such circumstances, a woman who initially has a pimp to herself usually becomes disturbed with the thought of having to share him with wife-in-laws (other women in the stable), due to the thought of possibly not receiving the full attention that she usually gets all by her lonesome. But a fast-paced pimp knows the risk of maintaining one hoe and one hoe only in his stable. It will bring the hoe to have a series of disoriented thoughts going through her mind.

Thoughts like wondering if you're really even capable of recruiting other women to work for you. Believing that her pimp's career is in her hands, and if she were to discontinue her services as his working prostitute, he would probably be assed out. And a few other similar thoughts.

That is why it is best to cover that from day one. To let her know that there will be more women who will come along to join the stable, and make sure that she understands all the benefits and advantages of having wife-in-laws. If it is set out upon her in a firm, comprehensive manner, then the woman will have no problem and will not second-guess or question the man's position of being the one who sets the rules.

Now here's a case with a pimp who meets the same exact materialistic criteria, but he has the advantage of having active prostitutes to show for. Most women who encounter him on grounds of orientation usually accept the invitation on giving the game a try upon his presentation, 'cause they see the other women in the stable whose functions and conduct equal to the man's confidence. If she observes the girls in the man's stable as happy and in high esteem, curiosity will allow her to want to see if she too can be brought to that frame of mind by dealing with this man under those circumstances.

She's already seasoned—meaning sexually promiscuous. So the hard part about getting her to accept the concept of prostitution isn't even the matter. All that matters now is if she likes what is being presented to her, and if she's willing to disregard all the less important things pertaining to her life, and become a part of a solid foundation. Seeing that other girls have willingly accepted the program given to them by the man in charge, she will automatically feel a sense of security and know that her confidence can always be reassured through one of her wife-in-laws when she needs it from a woman's perspective.

A pimp of that status or the other would usually be described as "reputable." He is mostly known as a successor, and a bad day of his would be irrelevant, and probably left unheard of. He has the tools to back up his status. Coming, being, and remaining equipped is a big advantage in the game.

There is also a flip side to that scenario. There may be a pimp who has a lot of knowledge and wisdom in regards to the game. However, he may not receive all the benefits that his skill entitles him to in the beginning, due to a misfortune that was brought on by a temporary setback in his life for one reason or the other.

All he may be maintaining in his life at the moment may be a hotel-motel room. A minimized wardrobe that keeps him from wearing the same outfit two days in a row from week to week. And keeps an average of $300 in his pocket. A pimp of this status has to enforce his skills three times harder than a pimp of the status that I previously described. He will be the one to experience several girls that will come and go from his program, before he gets one who stays and contributes to his status being escalated.

The kind of girl who stays down for him is more than likely the one who likes him him, and wouldn't mind being the one to take pride in him elevating. His companion, motivation, counseling, and inspiration are enough for her not to be interested in what another pimp, or any other man's program, is like. She has her own insecurities of possibly not being compatible with other guys, and she appreciates the feeling of being needed. She accepts and loves this man 'cause he's everything she wants in a guy. Nothing can make her feel more better than knowing that she's responsible for her man's financial status being up to par.

Besides, if she's been around the block a few times, either with other pimps, sugar daddies, Caption-Save-a-Hoe tricks, or any other type of man who was financially set, then she already knows that that type of story ends the same way it began. She comes with nothing, serves her purpose while she's there, and then leaves with nothing when it's all said and done. Back to square one. So now she knows that there's an opportunity for her to be appreciated for more than just being someone's "hot piece of ass" on demand.

Also, a pimp in this situation cannot have the same attitude, as far as arrogance, as one of higher status. A pimp who is all the way set can afford to have subtractions in his empire from time to time, 'cause it can be made up before the seriousness of it takes any actual effect. But for the pimp who's just getting the ball rolling, minor things can be brought about and arrogance can have a major effect on his program.

For example, he may find himself hanging around with crowds of other pimps, and monitoring their status—which is normal 'cause everybody learns and picks up ideas from one another. But let's say there's two of his partners in particular that he rolls with, and deep down in his heart he feels he has more pimpin' with him (knowledge of the game) than his partners do. But what's bothering him is the fact of how he's always in the passenger side of one of his partners' car 'cause he doesn't have one of his own.

One of the rings that his partner is wearing is worth more than what his one hoe could make off of flat backing in a month. And while he's stuck with one hoe, his pimp partners are keeping an average of at least three or four girls in their stables.

So his own arrogance and impatience will cause him to take no regard to the fact of how his partners took the correct route through the DMV to get a driver license so they can operate a vehicle legitimately. Or how their jewelry, plus whatever else they have on value and their three or four active prostitutes working as a strong team did not come over night.

No one stepped into the game on top! Unlike any other game in the underworld, there isn't a certain amount of money that someone can use to buy his or her way into being a certified pimp! So whatever current situation a pimp might be in, a high percentage of other pimps have been there as well.

But he may not want to see it that way. All he knows is that he has more pimpin' with him than them niggas, and he has to zoom past them—or at least catch up. Of course he isn't going to go over that matter with his partners. That would be a bit on the sensitive side, coming from one who is supposed to be a pimp. So who's the first person he takes the matter up with? His one hoe. The way an arrogant pimp would address her would be somewhere along these lines . . .

"Yeah, bitch. You know, pimpin gotta get deep around this muthafucka! The game doesn't revolve around no one hoe. I got partnaz out there who got three or four bitches that don't even look half as good as you, and they're doing it real big. Something isn't right!"

If that one hoe has been putting in an honest and productive effort on a constant basis, then a lecture like that will cause her to feel like he's trying to shift some of himself blame on to her, and this will automatically cause her to put up a defense.

Once the pimp realizes that he's risking a loss that he cannot afford to take, he'll justify the matter to his one hoe to set things back at ease. 'Cause reality will set in on him that he isn't going to receive any benefits by being impatient.

Although the bargain may seem rough, the reality is this: the main ones who become successors in the game are the ones who avoided doing time and being caught up in the justice system. And the ones who don't develop a drug habit. Doing time has always played its role in pimps having to start from scratch. In any street game, success comes with time. The most pimping that a person can do from behind bars is justifying the game to the misconceived and ignorant critics that a pimp encounters on a daily basis.

However, he is getting absolutely no credit in the area where it's most important—the game itself!

Obstacles

A pimp has the same amount of direct enemies, as he does indirect enemies. And each one of them holds an equal amount of threat to his empire. In order for a pimp to stay free from these, one must study and understand them beforehand, and also teach his women about the possible occurrence of each one, so when she encounters any of them, her response will be equivalent to one of experience, instead of vulnerability.

A pimp's key tool in the existence of his title is his hoe. With one, or however many his skill allows him to maintain, he is on the road to manifesting his goal. Without one, or any, is like a drug dealer without some product. The two main enemies that a pimp has who soar about like vultures and take any available opportunity to strike at the women who serve his purpose are . . .

The law officials and other pimps! In every major city in the United States that's known for prostitution-related activity, there are police departments that assign a particular division to deal with prostitution and prostitution-related matters such as, but not limited to, tricks and potential johns, pimps, obtainers, and relevant drug matters. A pimp who practices taking cautions knows when it is best for him to be, and when it is best for him not to be, present at this type of scene.

The police will make him a first preference as a target in this type of environment. But since police know that pimps are aware of this, they go for their next best alternative—his working prostitute! Police who are familiar with a certain area that they been assigned to for a significant amount of time know which prostitutes are out there working for pimps, and which ones aren't. When they have a choice of which caliber of a prostitute to take down, they'll rather go after the ones that work for pimps. Common sense tells them that it will have an effect on the pimp to one extent or the other. So they do it out of spite.

Subconsciously, some officers may feel that by enforcing their authority on prostitutes that work for pimps, they're making a statement that will eventually lead to pimping and prostitution-related activity in that particular community coming to a halt. But the chances of that happening are equivalent to the war on drugs being won. Some things are how they are, and pimping and prostitution is one of them.

As I already mentioned, the second most direct enemy to a pimp is indeed another pimp! For someone that is not familiar with the game, that would seem a bit unordinary, but it's true. What more could a pimp want from a new recruit that comes along in his stable, than one who is already seasoned and accustomed to paying a pimp? Hell, that saves him a lot of work. All that will be left up to him would be to customize his new hoe into meeting the requirements of his particular program, then take it from there.

Technically, a pimp losing a hoe under these circumstances poses more of a threat to him than losing her on any other grounds. Once she's been got by a seasoned pimp, she will then be in the presence of one who has the psychological capabilities of making her disregard any emotional attachments, feelings, memories, or care for the well-being of the pimp she was formerly with. Then to top it off, if she feels that the new program she's under is more suitable for her, in her mind she will look back on former incidents, circumstances, and predicaments she's been in, in comparison to her new pimp and his program and find herself having a feeling of hatred toward the mentioning of her former pimp's name.

Not to say that the same fate doesn't wait for the pimp that she may currently be with, due to the transitions of a woman's feeling and decisions. That's why a pimp places this expectation on a woman the second he initiates her into his stable. (As I mentioned in the answer to question number 15 in the "Stereotypes, Opinions, and Myths" section.)

The only exceptional circumstance where a pimp may consider not sweating a hoe in an effort to recruit her is if she belongs to a pimp partner of his, and he's more than happy to see him with the hoe, instead of without her. However, this exception is limited! If that hoe, who is being spared from being sweated by whichever friend or partner of her particular pimp, has lost characteristics in her conduct as a hoe, and that "out of pocket" activity is in favor of, or leaning toward this other pimp, then he will see himself being left with no choice but to do what is in his nature and knock his own partner for the bitch.

In a situation like that, it shouldn't be taken to heart. The bitch was more than likely silly to begin with. She was bound to be knocked by someone eventually. The respect that a hoe has for her pimp will reflect in her actions.

The other limited exception is where a pimp may be in a situation where he has to go off and do some time. His immediate pimp partners will probably be the only source of foreign pimpin' that his hoe(s) will be somewhat familiar with; and truth of the matter is, if he's going to be away for a while, the chances of them actually staying down for him all the way until his return into society are slim to nothing. Regardless of what their intentions are in the beginning—or until they get over the shock!

His own partners will feel that it would be best to recruit them, so that way the torch will still be burning as it's passed on (a hoe remaining in the game), instead of making a decision with unmanaged emotions and get with some square type of dude, then develop a regretful type of hatred toward pimps.

But overall, it's a pimp's responsibility to develop and maintain a strategic, philosophical lecture to share with any and all of the women that work under his basis. That way, the precautionary embedded in their minds will transgress against the possibility of them being got by the law or another pimp.

I am now going to share with you some of the indirect enemies that a pimp has. I say indirect 'cause they didn't choose to be who they are. Like how a pimp chose to be a pimp, and how an officer chose to be an officer. But rather they are natural enemies, due to their lust, selfishness, and greed. The way they pose a potential threat to a pimp is by being one who constantly tries to take a woman in the game, and turn her focus toward them for their own sexual gratification, or simply to fulfill their loneliness. And what makes it even worse, they believe they can buy a woman's soul, love, and honor with their fortunes. If this same kind of woman were to be brought back to the earlier state in her life before she became sexually promiscuous, and were to have been approached by this same type of dude, he wouldn't have a chance in hell at even getting a phone number out of her.

But now, here he is, and there she is. Accepting reality for what it is! This guy has her pimp beat by a long shot, as far as wealth and materialistic things. Let's say, for example, he's a fellow who's in high position at his job. His yearly salary is $200,000. He has stocks and investments in all kinds of property.

Hell, he even owns a business or two! He's been on the back burner of this hoe's mind since the first time she dated him as a client in her line of duty. Her pimp is more than happy every time he knows that she's about to go handle some business with this guy as one of her regulars, 'cause she usually comes back with about $500 after only a couple of hours.

What he doesn't know is how this sucker done been all up in that bitch's ear. More than likely after she opened up that door by half-heartedly confessing to having a pimp, by saying something like, "Well, I do work for somebody," giving him something to elaborate on during his many indentations for her to be basically bought by him as a wife. His overall invitation will usually fall somewhere along these lines:

"Now listen here, my darling. You are a very beautiful, smart, and ambitious young lady. You can be doing a whole lot more with your life than living to serve someone who really doesn't care about you. If that guy of yours that you work for really cared about you, he wouldn't have you indulging and interacting with strangers. Who's to say that some other guy that you meet, opposed to myself, isn't some kind of maniac who would only inflict harm upon you?

"Which is a strong possibility in your line of business?

"Then why not leave the person that you work for? His days of mourning for you will be short, if at all. And you will quickly be replaced by some other young lady who will come along to fill your shoes, 'cause he will be looking at it from a business perspective. Besides, women to him are looked at as nothing more than a product in his line of work.

"I am hereby today giving you the opportunity to no longer have to work as a prostitute, or a call girl. To no longer have to live in the transgression state of the woman being the one to be treated like a queen, while the man—a real man like myself—does all the work. Sweetheart, you will not have any disappointments if you only accept my sincerity, along with this offer. 'Cause as I look into your eyes, I can see something there that's telling me that you're really not happy with your life, and if you had a chance to live according to your original intentions, this would be the last thing on your agenda."

Now if that hoe hasn't been laced with the heads up and precautions of that type of approach, she would by then had tears forming in her eyes. Besides, this dude deserves an Oscar, plus a Golden Globe Award for the best bullshiter of the year! Once he's under the impression that his words are penetrating, he will go in for the grand finale.

"Listen, you deserve it to yourself, more than you probably even realize an opportunity at the finer things in life. As you already see, I am financially set, and all I need is a woman to share all of this with. I can retire today, and I'll still have enough money to last me until the end of my days. You will have to do nothing more than join me as my significant other, and I will fulfill your life in all the areas that men were absent, which I believe lead to you believing that your current occupation was your only alternative. I could be wrong, but that is what my heart is telling me.

"This coming weekend, I will be taking a two-week vacation in Hawaii. I would love for you to join me. If by any chance it will interfere with regular schedule, then I would suggest that you would accept the opportunity as the beginning of a new life with me, and putting your old life, including whoever you're involved with, behind."

As I was saying earlier, if that hoe wasn't laced or schooled about the science of that type of encounter, then it will pose a threat to her pimp. As soon as lil' mama comes back in from that date with that $500, all that's going to be lingering in her mind is a way out. It's partially her fault for not knowing any better, but it's more so her pimp's fault for not teaching her any better—that's if he knew himself!

So what usually happens in a situation like this—all while she's trying as hard as she can to see her man as nothing more than a monster—she's planning on using the next conflict that she gets into with him as her token (excuse) to make her move with Mr. Buy a Bitch, and remain as guilt free as possible.

So here's the routine: conflict occurs, hoe slips off. Pimpin' waits for the phone call to get served some news from another pimp that might have the hoe—doesn't happen. Pimpin' calls the jailhouse to see if she may have caught a hoe case—negative. And last, but definitely not least, it sets in that the hoe is nowhere to be found. Reason being, she's missing in action with Mr. Buy a Bitch in Hawaii, sipping on a smooth blended beverage out of a coconut. But she'll be back, and let me tell you why.

Due to the fact that Mr. Buy a Bitch met the woman on the grounds of being a client to her services as a prostitute, chances are, she's not the first prostitute he's encountered with on a tricking basis. Furthermore, she's probably not the first one who received the "I'm Mr. Right, and your pimp is Mr. Wrong, so come give me a try" invitation either.

As sweet as his words may sound, and as smooth as his charm may seem, why would a man in his 30s or 40s, who's successful in the corporate world and financially set, have an esteem to shout out that he's willing to take a prostitute he picked up on the streets into his home. Wouldn't a guy like that be expected to have a wife or a steady girlfriend? The kind you see in the movies attending an expensive, high-priced auction. Or dancing in a ballroom with a long $4000 dress on, with a pearl necklace that's worth more than a two-story West Coast project building that a hood nigga grew up in.

Or is it that he was married and did have that type of woman. But now he's separated or divorced, and his confidence has been knocked so far in the dirt that he believes that the only chance of a woman ever appreciating him again is if he can buy her off the streets and be viewed by her as someone who saved her life. Or is that what he calls himself doing as a cover-up for the fact that he enjoys seeing what his money can buy. If he believes that buying a woman off the streets is a good alternative for a divorce, he's got another thing coming!

Ninety percent of matters that lead up to divorce had something to do with betrayal and distrust. Now how the hell is a man going to be able to trust a woman that is knowingly seventy-two hours fresh out of a career as a prostitute? On that note, how can this woman he just took in live up to his expectations as a husband figure, trust him?

Besides, she knows from firsthand experience that he's into picking up prostitutes. And last, but definitely not least, him being in the matured adult age range, how would his fatherly instincts react if he had a daughter who he knew was a prostitute, and he had long ago disowned her? Then one day she pops up at his doorstep with some oddball, square type of dude and hits him with this.

"Yes, Dad, I just wanted to let you know that I've sincerely changed my life. And I owe it all to this guy right here. We been together for six months now, and he started off as being one of my regulars, but after a while I noticed how he was so sweet, and he offered to help me out. So here we are."

He would probably kick her ass for bringing some shit like that to his door. Then kick the guy's ass just for knowing that he's one of the many guys who's invaded his daughter's kitty cat, just 'cause it was for sale. I'll tell you, those tricks have a lot of monkey business with them!

A seasoned hoe that is familiar with this type of individual and all that comes along with them would probably see him as a perfect candidate to be robbed the first opportunity she gets. Then bring that jackpot home to her true love. But the one who isn't seasoned can fall victim to the distraction that this trick intends.

So now, with all these potential and susceptible strikes that Mr. Buy a Bitch has against him, it won't be long before he and the hoe that he mentally abducted from the game will have a fallout, due to either one, some, or all of the aforementioned scenarios placed into his character. His wealth and fortune will become of no importance to her, and his lame and unimpressive ways will not impress her one bit.

Then she, like many in the game before her, will experience the nonbeneficial involvement with this kind of guy, and find her way back to her pimp, or an environment that she can feel comfortable being herself in. Overall, matters like that can easily be avoided, as long as the woman is taught beforehand. There is a pimp phrase that states, "Proper instructions brings proper production!" And that phrase is relevant to the scenario that I just described.

Those Mr. Buy a Bitch situations aren't always brought about from guys of high status and financial stability. They can come in all shapes, forms, and sizes. It can be the neighborhood drug dealer. The security guard of a residential building, market, or shopping place. The desk clerk or employees of a hotel or motel. Or simply the guy from around the way that welcomes any hoe that wants to come over and use his place as a rest haven or hideout.

All of them are extras in the big picture. They have always been there, and will always be there. They are what would be commonly described as "in the way," without even realizing it. But any woman who has a strong will in obeying her pimp's instructions will not allow herself to be distracted by these oblivious figures.

Another key factor that is in the category of an indirect enemy to a pimp is a lesbian. Yeah, they probably aren't as common as most of the other direct and indirect enemies that I've mentioned, but they do exist. Obviously, they don't like men. But when it comes to a pimp, they have a particular vendetta. And what makes them a potential threat is the fact that they possess a great deal of cleverness and influence. Not as much as a pimp, but much more than any trick, or Mr. Buy a Bitch kind of guy. They each have their own personal reason for their sexual preference.

Some realized at a younger stage in life that they were attracted to women more than men. Others have had plenty of experience with men, but felt throughout a period of time that they would be better off in a relationship by being the dominant one.

Some have been turned out through experimenting, and they enjoyed the soft, sensual touch of a woman, as opposed to men. And you even got those who go both ways. Some of this kind are into prostitution. They'll have sex with men day in and day out, but only on the grounds of a consensual exchange for their services. Sex with men to them is very superficial. They feel that it is every man's place to carry on the position as a common trick. And any man who does more than that, especially pimps, is doing too much. The only person that they will allow themselves to be involved with on a relationship basis is indeed another woman.

They have a certain outlook on women with pimps. They believe that if a woman has a low-enough self-esteem to allow themselves to grow accustomed to the standards of being a prostitute and having a man to give all her money to, then she more than likely can be shifted in a direction away from the pimp, and cater to the desires of this lesbian. A lesbian will be stern and upfront with her influential approach.

"Shit! I'll be dammed if I give a man a muthafuckin thing after I done turned a trick. No disrespect to your nigga, or whatever, but a pimp is a sorry excuse for a man. That's just my personal opinion. All you got is a muthafucka who tells you what to do. You got to go out and get money for him to take care of you. You can do that for your damn self. Then he puts his hands on you and calls himself chastising you, like your some kind of child or something. Shit, you'z a grown ass woman. You don't need to be letting no nigga put his hands on you.

"He is doing that shit to stroke his own ego. That's why I don't fuck with men now. I'll end up killing me a muthafucka. Look, girl, I don't know if you're with dude 'cause you find the little pimp and hoe thing that yawl got going on as your only means of support. But if he got you thinking that you can't make it without him, that's bullshit! Ain't anybody in this neighborhood ever know me to have a man. But one thing that they can tell you is, 'That bitch don't need for nothing.' What I can do for you is put you up on some of these credit card schemes I be pulling, and a few other things. But the first thing you must do is let ol' boy go. Have him find some other bitch who likes that pimp shit. I need a little cutie on my team any way. Think about it, girl. After you done put in all that work, you gotta ask him for what you want. To me, a pimp ain't nothing but a spoiled trick!"

Sounds good, doesn't it? Well, it'll sound even better to that hoe if she isn't hip to what this kind of woman is hitting her with. I'm sure that at the time of this lesbian approaching this pimp's property, she doesn't have a stable woman.

Why? She doesn't want one. She's a swinger in her own way. The door to her home is a revolving one, as far as women who come to be in a relationship with her. The mentality of the lesbian I described is apparently the kind who leads the way when it comes to another woman being with her.

She ain't looking for no "little cutie" to be on her team. What she's looking for is another girl she calls herself running through, and then gets rid of her when the shit gets old. (Which usually doesn't take too long.) Her egotistical characteristics are similar to a man's. You know, the kind who has sex with as many women as he can so he can feel good about himself.

But being able to tamper with a pimp's empire, plus have another girl chalked off as a "been there, done that" would really make her day. She will feel good about herself, feeling that she outsmarted a pimp. Even owners of brothels (whorehouses) do not allow lesbians to come inside 'cause they already know that they have exploiting related intentions.

The blind can't lead the blind, and a woman cannot serve a productive acquaintance with another woman. It is a transgression against the laws of nature. The only time a pimp would allow a woman that works for him to indulge in same-sex activity is if she is getting paid for it on the grounds of business, or if it's involving one of her wife-in-laws. Other than that, it is prohibited. The old saying has it: "A woman really knows how to satisfy another woman." But truth be told, there is no other object on the face of the earth that can substitute for the man's penis, which is the vagina's intended companion.

Another indirect enemy of the pimp would be the gangster. Of course, the ones he doesn't know personally. Since there are a lot of pimps who have, at one time or another in their lives, familiarized themselves with that lifestyle to one extent or the other. When the topic is discussed by a gang member in regard to a pimp, one of the things that is usually mentioned is, "Why them pimp niggas be telling their hoes not to fuck with no gangsta niggas? Are they afraid that a gangsta nigga might take their bitch from them!"

To answer that question, no! If anybody other than a pimp happens to gain possession of a hoe, it won't take long before their incompatibilities take effect, and everyone goes their separate ways. That's the least of pimp's worries. However, in the particular business of pimping and prostitution, there are certain guidelines that a hoe will be instructed to follow in order to avoid misconducts and malfunctions during her line of duty.

Any hoe that has been properly instructed will have an automatic instinct to do the best she can to screen a potential client that approaches her at any time, anywhere. The things she has to remain on high alert of are the following: Other pimps besides her own. Police officers in an undercover capacity. And people who would more than likely become a problem. And an unsuccessful date if she were to attempt to follow through with that person.

Gangbangers happen to fall under the last example I just gave. Not only black gangbangers, but Hispanic ones as well. There aren't very many hoes that have been in the game for a while, who hasn't experienced an unsuccessful date with a gangbanger. What usually happens is, the gangbanger will receive everything sexually that was agreed upon at the beginning of the deal. But the whole time, he has devious thoughts going through his head such as, "I ain't no muthafuckin' trick! This hoe got me fucked up, if she thinks I'm about to let her go on about her way with my money." Then at the end of that episode, he forcibly takes the money back."

Now she's worried that if she has to go back to her pimp and tell him that, she has to deal with the chances of his reaction if he doesn't believe her. But if she keeps it to herself and proceeds to make up for it, it would have been considered time wasted.

There are several different incidents in which a hoe has gone, and can go, through by dealing with guys in a gangbanging mentality while she's working. Things like not being let out of a hotel-motel room upon her request. And the same matter from a vehicle. Robbed for her cell phone and her earnings that she has not turned in yet. And last but not least, find herself in the midst of an unexpected crowd of guys, in which she knows she will not win or have any defense in the matter if these guys decide to take total advantage of her.

This is the reputation that gangbangers have, as far as their encounter with hoes. Specifically the ones who are on the hoe stroll, looking for a prostitute to pick up. As for a prostitute who has a pimp, every shift that they work, they are in hopes of not coming across any life-threatening, terrifying, or time-wasting situations. Besides, gangbangers don't meet the expectations that a hoe looks for in a trick anyway. A hoe is looking for the kind of fellow who is humble and willing to do a fair exchange, no-robbery deal, in a price range somewhere between $50 to $150 just for a few minutes of her time. Now how many active gangbangers are known to meet that criteria? Not too many. A hoe doesn't see a gangbanger as a trick, any more than he sees her as one. Therefore, he has no beneficial or productive use to a prostitute in her line of duty.

And finally, the main figure that poses the biggest threat to a pimp that has drug addict hoes—a drug dealer! There isn't any other figure that can be found in any general environment that a drug addict woman would preferably want to be with than a drug dealer. If this is the type of woman that a pimp (a sober pimp at that) is dealing with, then he has a hell of a job on his hands.

First of all, any drug addict hoe that works for a drug-free pimp is more than likely attractive enough for a trick, or anyone in general not to notice that she uses. (Not right offhand.) In simpler terms: the bitch looks good! And unless she exposes her business, as far as being an addict, some may not ever know. Especially the ones that work for a reputable pimp. He may not want people to see him as a "drug addict's girl pimp."

There is a particular blend of recipe that a pimp has to be very precise with in order to maintain, financially exploit, and manage this caliber of a woman. He will have to develop a method, which will keep his women looking no farther than him for dependency of their habit being supported. And still be able to gain profit from her work as a prostitute, after budgeting money that has to go back into her habit. Excessively be in a state of lecturing and explaining to keep this kind of woman from dating drug dealers for drugs. Being stuck somewhere while getting high with tricks. And accepting a drug dealer's offer to be taken in by him on an "I can support your habit" basis.

Once this type of woman has had plenty of those kinds of offers presented to her by a drug dealer (who doesn't try very hard 'cause his product does all the talking for him), she will then begin to weigh out what she believes to be options to herself. And the main thing she will be concentrating on is the fact that she has to work and perform to just about the same standards as any other hoe in general that works for a pimp.

But for what? To belong to a man who specializes in managing prostitutes, and allow him to take care of her habit. If getting high is more important to her (90 percent of most cases) than sharing the goal with her man to get rich, then the two of them see life out of two totally different windows.

She'll visualize the alternative concept of laying up under one man—the drug dealer, of course—and go no farther than sexually entertaining him to be well taken care of, as opposed to a pimp who is going to work her till her heels fall off. A pimp who deals, or has dealt, with a drug addict hoe knows within himself what the chances of losing her under those circumstances are every time she is out of his sight.

Unlike any other precautionary lecture that a pimp would usually give his woman about the potential threats and distractions that come along in the game, he would have to disregard going over the truth of the matter with this kind of hoe. Drug addicts are known to see if a person is bluffing, and take no chances. (Due to the drug being so compelling—especially crack, methamphetamine, and heroin.)

A pimp would have a better chance of getting compliance by placing fear into this kind of hoe.

"Okay, bitch! I don't know who the fuck you might take me as, but don't think that by me accepting you for having a habit is a gateway opened for you to get beside yourself and venture off into finding someone who sells this shit, then get to thinking that he's the one you might be interested in. 'Cause I'm gonna let you know now—any bitch that's a product of me, which happens to be you, is not going to allow herself to be bought by this bullshit, if there's anything I can do to stop it.

"And just in case you might want to entertain the thought of being with one of them dope-dealing boys and think you might be safe with him, guess what? I might do something to both of you muthafuckers 'cause can't no drug dealer walk around here with the pride and joy of feeling like he knocked a real live pimp for a real fine bitch, just 'cause he sells what you get high off of.

"Now there isn't and never will be a time where I'll fall short of making sure that you're well taken care of. Just as long as you continue to do what you've been doing. With my mind and your body, we can get somewhere, and always have something to show for. But with a drug dealer's product, and your body, he won't get nothing but two things—a nut, and tired of you. Where will that eventually leave you? Wondering why you just had to try something else, when you already had the best you can get, but you refused to see it.

"In this particular case with me and you, I'm not going to even let shit go that far. 'Cause I already told you what I'd do. Now if you take heed to what I'm saying, and hang around long enough, you'll learn to appreciate me and be glad I brought this matter to you like this, so you can avoid a whole lot of disappointments that you'll be seeing other bitches going through, instead of yourself."

Now a lecture somewhere along those lines may be one of the best ones to cause a drug addict hoe to have second thoughts about getting with a drug dealer, which is always going to be very tempting. The truth of the matter is this here. As I already mentioned, a drug dealer poses the biggest threat to a pimp who has women that get high. But it also depends on the status of the drug dealer!

If he's a small-time dealer, for example, who sells at the lowest level of the game, which is the street level, he will only take in a hoe that gets high off his product for no longer than seventy-two hours. Why? Well, when she first walks through the door, both of them will be ignorant to the fact of how long this is actually going to last.

On the first day, he will be thinking that he scored a really cool bitch. And while he's feeling high, he'll probably be indulging in several sexual activities throughout the day and night. He thinks he'll be able to afford it, so he'll have no problem tossing her what she asks for upon her request.

Day number two: He'll find his hustler instinct kicking in, telling himself that he can't put too much trust in her, or turn his back on his product around her. Or even brandish it in front of her. He'll start catching on that "the more she sees, the more she'll want."

Day number three: She'll begin to show signs of deficiency as far as the guys desire to have sex at his will. And to top it off, she won't be able to take no for an answer when she wants to get high. It will start to dawn on dude really hard, the thought he tried to avoid the day before—that feeding this fiend has tapped into his profit. And not only that, but she's in the way of other girls that he's used to dealing with. Now with all these disadvantages pending, due to her, he notices that she's extra luggage that he would rather not carry. While the tension is thick between the two of them, he kicks her out with no remorse.

He was a small-time street dealer, who tried to live above his financial standards, and he's mad at the bitch, instead of himself. In most common situations, a drug dealer of this status would be the only type that a hoe with a pimp would have any knowledge of. The threat that he poses to a pimp would be appropriately described as a "temporary distraction," 'cause that hoe will come back to pimpin'.

Okay. Now here's the sugar-daddy type of drug dealer. These ones are usually in the age range of their late 30s and up. Most of the time, they are foreigners who speak very little English or at least have an accent. Their status as a drug dealer is a couple of steps above the typical aforementioned street dealer. They usually sell weight or quantity. Their door usually stays opened to at least one or two drug addict hoes. He has a better skill of dealing with them and developing a longer acquaintance, as opposed to the typical street dealer that was fascinated by the "cheap sex" opportunity.

These sugar-daddy dealers are mature to the matter that these kinds of women are hoes. He puts up no objection to them going out and doing what they feel needs to be done. As a matter of fact, he encourages it. It saves him a buck or two. To her, his home is viewed more as a rest haven. She keeps a portion of her clothes and belongings there so she can come freshen up, then go as she pleases.

She may or may not have a key to that residence, and all that the sugar daddy is happy with is the ability of having access to a sexual companion. She will not develop any emotional feelings for him, and he doesn't want or expect her to.

If ever a fallout was to occur between the two of them, it will more than likely be caused by something coming up missing. The way this kind of individual poses an unintentional threat to a pimp is, he will always remain the hoe's next best option. Once the hoe develops access and acknowledgment of one of these types of guys, she will not hesitate to act out in a defiant manner on her pimp's basis. Knowing that she may have an alternative as far as "stability" and having her habit supported.

And third, and probably the most kind of threatening kind of figure to a pimp in the drug dealing department, I would have to say is the boss-figure dealer. These fellas—mostly of some Hispanic descent or the other, and in the same age range as the aforementioned sugar daddy—has a status in the world of narcotics that is far beyond any dealer that people on the streets or around the hood would be personally familiar with.

For a drug addict hoe to encounter one of these guys would be entirely coincidental, and in her line of duty. Him being able to support her habit would be no problem. These types of guys have a subconscious fetish to see how far women will go for their product. If, by any chance, he happens to take an actual liking toward the hoe, and decides to bring her home to keep (which will be somewhere far away from where she's a familiar face at) then her pimp, and the game can kiss that hoe good-bye!

The basis that an ordinary hoe would fall out with a Mr. Buy a Bitch kind of guy is totally different with a drug addict hoe and her big-time dealer. He doesn't expect her to be an angel, but at the same time, he's guaranteed to have it his way with her as long as he has an unlimited supply of what she lives for—getting high!

As far as her, on the other hand, she will not be skeptical about any of his conduct 'cause her habit is being taken care of, and all else is not important. She can possibly serve this man as a shadow, or an arm piece, for a significant amount of time and be missing in action from the game for quite a while. But it'll still be in her.

While some pimps have very little or no experience with this caliber of a hoe, there are others who specialize in them. Then there are those who even try their luck with having both them, along with sober hoes at the same time. For one to maintain this type of woman, he must include a high tolerance in his person.

There are only two circumstances in which a pimp would allow a woman of his that gets high, to turn a trick with a drug dealer. The first one is, if the pimp himself is drug free, he would be more than happy to see one of his hoes have a drug dealer as a client that gives her a large quantity of the product all in one date. That way it will hold him back from having to come out of his pockets with cash to buy it for her.

And the second one is, if the pimp happens to be one who gets high himself, chances are his hoe is already accustomed to dating drug dealers 'cause he encourages it. Her coming back from a date with some of the substance that both of them use is just as good as coming back with money.

The pimping and prostitution that is done on the street level will always remain available for the direct and indirect enemies that I have noted in this section. Most of them go hand in hand with the environments that serve as hoe strolls, such as truck stops, areas near strip clubs, drug-infested areas, areas near adult bookstores, areas where tourists pass through, and long strips where there are several hotels and motels.

A lot of pimps would prefer to elevate their game from the concrete to the carpet. For anyone who doesn't know what that means, the concrete is the track, where they all get famous at. And the carpet is an alternative, which will allow streetwalking to be modified, to eliminate some of the nonbeneficial encounters that hoes go through.

Final Thought

There was a time in history when the pimp game stood out as being common. Today, however, the game is on sacred grounds. It is not for everybody to know. The less people to know a certain pimp as one, the better off it is for him. That is one of the major effects that took effect in the game throughout the years. Some changes that came along in the game were for the better. Cellular telephones were a big advantage that brought convenience to means of communication. It made it easier for pimps and hoes to get things done outside of each other's physical presence, without having to use phone booths or pagers.

Another change that occurred for the better was the players. That's right. By the game constantly revolving with the participants, it's staying alive. While a lot thought that it died out a couple of eras ago, it only, as a matter of fact, got more popular. It was meant to appear as if it died down. That's why the pimps of today, as opposed to the pimps of yesterday, wear attire that is fly and up-to-date, but does not make them stand out apparently by their title. When they do wear an outfit that meets the expected pimp criteria dress code, it's done on occasions of special events.

A change that occurred for the worse was drugs. Particularly crack cocaine. Pimps who had hoes that only used heroin were able to maintain their stable 'cause they kept themselves as the only access to heroin that their hoes had. Plus, it isn't a consistent drug. Once the woman has had her fix, she can proceed with her agenda, since a heroin user's routine is only once every two to six hours. With crack cocaine, there is no satisfaction where a person will say to himself or herself that they "had enough." Nowadays, crack and heroin go together hand in hand like dots on dice. And that's why most drug-free pimps have drug-free girls as a first preference to work for them.

However, this method caused the game to be a bit more risky. Young hoes—young, meaning not eighteen years of age yet—play a major role in a lot of young pimps' stable. Most women who come out of a neighborhood who accepts a pimp's invitation to work for him as a prostitute would have been the same one to walk the path of becoming a drug addict if they would have remained in that neighborhood.

This also encouraged law officials to become involved with interfering in the pimp and prostitution trade, that way they can have a better arrest under their belts, when they bust someone for endangering the welfare of a minor. Police are very consistent with their efforts to make this kind of bust. They believe that a young lady's mind is vulnerable to the extent where they can feed her milk and cookies, brainwash the girl into believing that her pimp is a big ol' monster for having her work the streets. Then pick up the phone and call Mom to let her know that her daughter has been picked up for prostitution and she needs a legal guardian to come and pick her up from the police station—as soon as she tells them who her pimp is!

As you see, a pimp's job has become one that requires more skill and strategy than before. As far as the successors in the game, they live a luxurious life. Similar to a rapper's. Only, pimps don't pay income tax. Nobody likes pimps! Nobody. No one likes a pimp except for another pimp, and a hoe. People might respect the individual who happens to be the pimp, but that doesn't mean that they like him.

They'll respect him for another characteristic in his person besides being the pimp. It might be his generosity. It might be his childhood acquaintance with a person as old-time friends. It might be for his capabilities of holding a good conversation, or it might be him being a good advisor when someone is in need of some positive or productive feedback. It might be his capability of putting a smile on people's faces when he kicks some "pimp shit."

Yeah, they may smile, they may grin. But when it's all said and done, they still don't like him. If you took all of the most common participants that are found in the black underworld—the pimp, the prostitute, the pusher, the addict, the gangster, and the prisoner—and place each person from each one of those in front of your average person, then give him the wish for one of them to drop dead, free of charge, no murder case. guess which one that person will pick? The pimp.

Who is a pimp for somebody to dislike? Well, first, a person would have to know one to form an honest opinion about one. The general outlook on a pimp is him being a guy who is spoiled with firsthand company with the second thing a man values most in life next to his money—women. While some guys have a hard enough time wondering where their next shot of pussy is going to come from (a free shot at that), a pimp is beyond that 'cause he has a whole different use of the women he's in control of—for them to use their pussy to get him rich. He sees each of his women as a walking ATM, with a heartbeat!

So it should only be obvious that getting some pussy is the least bit of his worries. But like I said, that's the general opinion. Coming from a person's opinion that might actually know a pimp, to whatever extent, they'll place a mental boundary on where they stand with him as far as trust. They have more than likely witnessed the overall persona of his conduct with women, such as seeing how the pimp's women are very submissive to him (from a regular person's outlook). Seeing how his approach on women may be a lot bolder and achieved than his own. Having an ideal assumption of his source of income. His flamboyant, and arrogant conduct, and a few other characteristics that this regular person may feel offended by when it is going on in his presence, but doesn't really know why.

All that this guy might be certain of is that he has a pretty woman of his own, and even though him and the pimp has an all right rapport with one another, he still feels interfered with the thought of the pimp even laying eyes on her. It could be the fact of how this regular fellow had got acquainted with his woman with a simple approach by being himself. Now heres a pimp who's in arm's reach of the neighborhood, who has a vicious tongue, bold approach, and enough pick-up lines to start his own course at "Player's University."

Yeah, they're cool, but all the dude knows is that his woman better stay the hell away from him. Or it could be the opposite. It can be a dude that's acquainted with pimpin' on the same basis. Only thing is he may have an ugly bitch, no bitch, or has a hard time even getting a bitch! While he's witnessing pimpin's skills up close and personal, all he's wishing is that he acquires a portion of that skill, and he imagines what he would be able to accomplish in his loneliness with it.

You also got those who know a pimp on a personal basis, but they are clients to his girls. Even though they may try to appear to be unbothered, truth is the sight of his face turns their stomach. They're looking at the man to whom their money goes that they came out of their pockets with, just to have sex with the women that work for him. These types of people keep their fingers crossed for a pimp's downfall.

There's even some fellows who are local, and they have every want and desire to buy a piece of one of pimpin's girls, but their pride is in the way, and they don't want to join those who have to look at the man that's got their money.

There are several different reasons people don't like pimps. Reasons that are real. And reasons that are cover-ups for others. But for those who want to go on with the theory of a pimp being one who treats women bad, I got news for you that a hoe would probably be quicker to tell you before somebody else—many hoes need a man of that position! That's the bottom line. If people wouldn't allow themselves to feel disturbed with the concept of sex being a business, they wouldn't try to find something to say to knock it, or anything in regards to it.

What's Love Got to Do with It?

There are a couple of theories that have been floating around with the word *love* and its relevance to the game. Some say, "There is no love between a pimp and a prostitute." While other theories have it that "the game is based on love."

Well, my theory opposes to both of those to an extent. And agrees to both of those to another extent. First and foremost, hoes are not to be loved. It makes absolutely no sense for one to believe that they love something or someone who isn't promised to them the next day. Hoes are to be taken care of. Hoes are to receive emotional management, guidance, physiological therapy, care, concern, and counseling. Of course, from the person that they feel is best for the job—pimps!

But *love* is an inadequate feeling that would make no sense for a pimp to believe he has for a hoe. Most of all, it is not necessary. Regardless of how a pimp may be feeling about a hoe of his, they'll still get taken care of accordingly, in response to their conduct. As a man, a pimp doesn't have dysfunctional emotions, as the woman, which experiences mood swings and spontaneous change in conduct.

It is his job to monitor and analyze the woman, so he can skillfully know what action to take in order to set her mind back on track. So, therefore, the man deals with this caliber of woman with skill, not emotion!

Now, on the woman's behalf. It is within her nature to develop an emotional feeling for the person she's calling herself doing what she does for. It is easy for a woman to describe the least bit of attachment to somebody as love.

There're even guys who aren't, or don't even try to be pimpin any type of way who has experienced girls that are talking about they "love them" not even forty-eight hours into their relationship. As far as the feelings that a hoe tends to develop for her pimp, it would be more appropriately described as "infatuated." Meaning a transitory fondness! A feeling that comes with them and leaves with them. They will go through life feeling this way about several different men. And each one will be better than the previous one. (As far as they believe.)

The chances are, more than likely, a pimp will have the dominant place in a hoe's heart, as far as the person she had the deepest feelings for. But it is what it is as far as the true definition for the feeling. Hoes are not known to be ones to look intensively into matters. Where their thinking falls short, that's where a pimp picks up for them. And if *love* is the best interpretation that a hoe can come up with to describe their infatuated feelings toward their pimp, then so be it! Besides, it's the way that they feel about their man that's going to determine how they choose to perform when it comes time to do what their hand calls for in the name of the game.

For anyone who thinks that pimping is an easy task, and the successors are spoiled individuals who are living beyond the skills of their trade, then find a regular person, give him a rundown about all of the requirements and challenges that a pimp faces, and ask him if he'll take the job for a one-million-dollar-a-year salary.

Most fellas would have to pass on that one, 'cause it's obvious that it's a full-time job. A pimp pimps 24-7, 365 days a year, and 366 days on a leap year. If a person isn't willing to put down everything else in life to pick up on some pimpin', then it isn't even a matter of discussion.

The successors in the game have just what they deserve. 'Cause they were the ones who decided to put down all else and pick up on some pimpin' at one time or another in their lives. They live with the reality of the fact that their whole empire can crumble at the blink of an eye. But at the same time, they accept the fact that their fate and destiny is in their own hands. A pimp's major challenge is he verses his own strategy. A person giving himself the challenge to maintain a job that requires intellectual advancement on a daily basis deserves all the rewards he has coming!

In the 1960s and '70s, R&B and classic soul music has always made songs that had subliminal messages that were based on pimps, prostitutes, and heroin. Songs like "Bad Girls" by Donna Summers was strictly about prostitution. Raw and uncut. "King Heroin" by James Brown. And the whole soundtrack to the movie *The Mack.*

That was a time and era when black musicians shouted out the reality of the things that went on in the black underworld from the heart—not for the money.

Unfortunately, those days are gone, and we'll never get them back. With the exception of a couple of Southern California rappers, Bay Area rappers, and a couple of rappers from the South, a lot of rappers have been putting pimping in their mouths where it doesn't belong.

As a result to this, you got all kinds of brothers and others perpetrating. That's why a lot of people don't respect and acknowledge one's self-proclaimed title as a pimp upon first impression. When a lot of women, particularly hoes, get approached by a pimp on a fluke, they're unable to tell if it's some clown nigga that knows how to talk slick, or someone who is a certified pimp.

Her actions as a result of being unsure may not always be the appropriate reaction for that situation. But if she feels something isn't right, she'll feel it's a chance not worth taking. Nobody likes perpetrators. Not hoes, not pimps, not people in general!

Perpetrators have a lot to do with a real pimp being doubted at first sight. A person on the regular doesn't become convinced that a pimp is who he portrays to be, until they see him in action. Pimpin' isn't how pimpin' looks, walks, talks or acts. Pimpin' is what pimpin' does!

Unaware people always try to make a definition of what the word *pimp* stands for. First of all, when the word came about, it wasn't broken down in an abbreviated form—PIMP. It stands for what it is, and who it is. It does not stand for Paper In My Pocket, and all that silly shit. If one were to take the letters and abbreviate each one with a word, the most relevant phrase would be, "Professionals In Managing Prostitutes."

Or if PIMP were to come out of a hoe's mouth and land on a pimp's ears, all he would be interpreting from her is, "Please instruct My Pussy"!

There are only one set of rules to the pimp game. Just like there's one set of rules to the NBA. Each pimp pimps his own way individually, but stays within the guidelines of the rules in order to be an official productive member of the game. Same to a basketball player, in which all of them play with their own individual style and technique, but it doesn't exceed the guidelines of the rules.

Pimps are born. Hoes are made. And suckers are created! Nevertheless, pimps don't become successful by hesitating; they get there by demonstrating!

The Prostitute

Prostitutes! What would the world be without them? Lets see, the crime rate for sex offences would probably be sky high, due to the number of guys that would have to use rape as an alternative result of the misfortune of their not-so-good looks, lack of game, and confidence insecurities. The concept of pimping would have never been created. And women would have had to go through life without the advantage of how far their female companionship can get them, due to its value.

Since the beginning of time, the law of nature has allowed the female sex in all of the animal's kingdom (including humans) to be the desired one. That's why everyone has heard that "prostitution is the oldest profession." Because it is. It didn't take long for a woman to notice how she is unconditionally desired by the opposite sex, which gave her an idea of developing a strategy to use this to her advantage.

There are a large number of people who take offence, and are surprisingly disturbed with the concept of prostitution. This has also been around since the beginning of the trade as well. There are many passages and scriptures in the Bible that were documented back to those days, which shows how the world viewed them then. Such as Ezekiel 16: 23-34. The entire twenty-third chapter in the book of Ezekiel is a metaphor for two unholy countries that God was upset at—with prostitutes.

In the country of Samaria was a prostitute named Oholah. And in the country of Jerusalem was a prostitute named Oholibah.

Proverbs chapter 7:6-27. Hosea chapters 1 and 2. And even the book of Revelations had a scripture in its sevententh chapter sixteenth verse that states, "And the ten horns which thou sawest upon the beast, these shall hate the whore, and shall make her desolate and naked, and shall eat her flesh, and burn her with fire."

So that goes to show how long prostitution and the disturbed outlook a large portion of the world has always had on it. But why hate? Everybody is familiar with the general format of how the man can have multiple sex partners whether he's in a relationship or not, and it appears to be all right. Why? 'Cause maybe it's a statement being made that he's good in the area of getting a lot of girls.

And if he happens to be in a relationship with a woman, it's still no big deal 'cause he knows or believes that him having sex with other women will not affect the relationship between him and his own woman.

But as soon as there's a woman who's promiscuous, everybody is forming a negative opinion about her—especially by men—unless her promiscuity is in his favor. Or if the woman is in a relationship and she's having sex with other men besides her own and her boyfriend was to find out, his reaction would not be the same as the one he would expect, or want her to have if the tables were turned.

Men finding out about their women cheating on them has led to several acts of violence, suicides, murders, and imprisonment. Think about it in this aspect: Let's say the laws of nature were the other way around. The man was the unconditionally desired one. And women would walk through hell with gasoline drawers on just to get to a man due to their uncontrollable lust. And the male gender was known for committing acts of prostitution to female clients on a twenty-four-hour basis.

Can you imagine how many fellas would resort to this as a source of income? The crime rate would be down so low that there would be a Great Depression in all the criminal courts' economic system.

However, that example is only hypothetical, and it remains that women are the ones with that advantage—not men! That's why prisons are overfilled with men, while only a very small percentage of inmates are women. Prostitution has so many descriptions and forms, that it has become common in today's world. The phrase "sex sells" has a deeper meaning than someone understands the concept of it.

The most pleasing sight on earth to the man's eye is indeed a woman. Some would think it would be money, but what good is money to look at if it doesn't belong to you? Now, as far as a woman, whether she belongs to a man or not, her appearance can be interrupted in his mind in several different ways that can stimulate his sex drive.

Most television commercials that are advertising a product will have an attractive female modeling for the product to catch the viewer's attention. There was a time and era where people would flip through their TV while a commercial came on just to avoid it. But as the world gradually catches on to the power that the sight of a beautiful woman has, they'll put forth effort to include her in anything on the market.

The front cover of magazines, music videos, preview advertisements of movies—shit, a lot of times the woman you see in the previews only play in a small portion of the movie. But that's left for you to find out once you've seen it. All they're concerned about at the box office is the woman in the preview attracting you to the movie.

Even your everyday TV sitcom shows. What TV sitcom do you not know to have at least one attractive female as one of the cast members? Some guys watch a certain show just to catch a particular female actress that they enjoy seeing.

So that's an example of women and some of the advantages that they have when they allow themselves to be exploited on a harmless scale. But on a more intense note, let's move along into the world of prostitution as we picture it.

The most common term that is used to describe a prostitute is the word *hoe*. That word is a simplified spin-off that came from the word *whore*. When people entertain the thought of a prostitute, they think of a woman who is sexually immoral.

Women who use what they got to get what they want. It's common sense what a prostitute is. Everybody has seen one. If not on a direct basis, then on a basis where that person didn't know when he crossed a hoe's path. But they exist. Plenty of them. And the job gets done. Whether it's in a public restroom at a local bar, or while a girl is sitting on the bench of a bus stop to catch tricks. Whether it's in a crack house, or at a bachelor party being thrown on a private yacht. Whether it's done with directors nearby with cameras rolling, or done in an alley behind a church—it's done!

One of the things that linger in people's minds are why a woman would accept herself to become a prostitute. Well, first of all, it all depends on what caliber of a prostitute they are. And what extent they go through in regards to the classification of their trade. You got some women who are unconsciously prostituting, and you couldn't put a gun to their head to convince them of what they are. Then you got those who are sex fiends, and been one since the day they lost their virginity.

Probably due to a lack of self-effort and responsibilities, they just decided to be lazy in any case, since they have their pussy to fall back on. Some women are drug addicts with a costly addiction, and they try to tell themselves that if it weren't for the drugs, they wouldn't be hoes. But that's bullshit! If they were to sober up the next day, they would still need money and continue to get it the easiest way they know how. A woman doesn't have the stomach to be a prostitute one day, and then scorn it the next.

You got some women who allowed themselves to be easily turned out 'cause they felt it was an opportunity to be accepted by something that was bigger and better than what they were already doing. (Which was probably nothing.) Then you have some young ladies who turned their own selves out 'cause they had a very low self-esteem, and every opportunity they had to indulge with the opposite sex (males), they didn't let it pass them by. They had their own insecurities, and the more men they have sex with helped balance that insecurity for them.

By the time they got to a certain age in life where they would have to be self-reliable as far as finances, prostitution to one degree or another was not a hard option for them. Then there's those who may have been discussed with the thought of turning a trick at one point or another in their life, then came a time where the whole world was against them and the only emergency source of back up they had was their womanhood, and they felt the time was there to swallow their pride, and sell it.

You got some women who have been through different series of rape incidents in their lives, by either a direct family member or a distant one. By a neighbor, or by a schoolteacher. Whatever the case was, their minds at the young and vulnerable age of these occurrences was easily influenced into believing there was nothing wrong with the activity that was taking place between them, and whoever the guy was, and these secretive affairs became a burden that this woman has to carry until she enters the state of womanhood. Once she's old enough to realize that the secretive sexual affairs that were carried out between her and her molesters, she'll feel as if she had been robbed of her soul. She develops a certain outlook on all men, which causes her to feel like they owe her something for her attention, companionship, and time. She becomes an emotionless individual.

Activities such as kissing and holding hands are something they've excluded from their conduct. They are not interested in having a male companion to consider a significant other. If by any chance this type of woman ever happens to have a pimp, she will only see him as a necessity in the "stabilizing" part of his profession. As far as developing an emotional attachment toward him is totally out of the question. The only thing possible that she could become attached to him for would be the reliability of his guidance—and a pimp wouldn't have a problem with that.

Futhermore, you got women who turn themselves out without even realizing what they're doing. It may be a time in their life where they find themselves in the need of help. And when they weigh out their options, they're stuck to one fella who has always made an assurance to the woman that he's available if she were to ever need him. This might be a guy who's way out of her league, and not someone she would be bothered with on the norm. But due to the situation that led up to her considering him, all the matters of how he looks, and what nationality and age he is becomes irrelevant.

She goes to him and allows herself to be taken care of on the grounds of having a sugar daddy. Most women become accustomed to this alternative, and find themselves becoming lazy. And I mean lazy on the grounds of them figuring that they can always fall back and rely on a man who's willing to take care of them, instead of working and depending on themselves.

Well, one sugar-daddy alternative leads to another. So what eventually happens without her realizing it is that instead of her relying on a sugar daddy on a long-term basis, she'll figure that there isn't much of a difference between them and some other guy that might be a stranger, but she can still serve him his purpose (sex) as well as he can serve her (money), and they can each go their separate ways without any strings attached.

What I have briefly shared with you are only a few ways, out of many, that women lead up to becoming a prostitute. Whether part time or full time, partial or whole. I'm now going to do a roll call of twenty-eight different kinds of hoes that exist in alphabetical order. Some of the characteristics that may be specified about one type of hoe can probably be found in many others as well.

1. Bottom Hoe

A bottom hoe is one who holds the title for remaining her pimp's longest running active prostitute. While other girls in a pimp's stable comes and goes on an often basis, a bottom hoe has always been there—to watch them come and go right alongside the whole time. As far as a "one hoe pimp," who purposely keeps one hoe with no intentions to accumulate others, his one hoe cannot be considered his bottom bitch—that is his only bitch!

Let's go to the concept of playing cards. Say, a person is playing a hand he was dealt. And throughout the game, his hand is constantly changing, as he's discharging and pulling new cards. There's one card in his hand that remains there throughout the whole game, while the stack that makes his hand go from thick to thin and everything in-between. Well, that one card for the person who is playing that hand is what a bottom hoe is to a pimp.

In many situations, bottom hoes have been the ones to bare their pimps' children. And the first ones that a pimp would allow throughout a period of time to handle other necessary, productive matters in their program besides prostitution.

2. Call Girl Hoe

A hoe that may be referred to by this title doesn't necessarily mean that she works for a tax-paying service. Any hoe who is seeing her clients in any other aspect besides walking up and down the street "car hopping" is more than likely doing everything as far as scheduling dates through telephones, cell phones, e-mail, voicemail, pagers, or a service dispatcher.

No doubt about it, it is a much safer alternative than streetwalking. However, all women do not have the time and patience to go to a legitimist service and wait for a clientele to build up.

A woman with a common communication tool, such as a cell phone, can easily build up her own clientele with people she deals with on her own basis. The only difference is, the clients that go through a service to get women are usually middle- to upper-class gentlemen, who come willing to pay top dollar for a woman.

Whereas a woman who doesn't go through a service just takes them as they come, 'cause tax paying kind of takes the fun away from hoes that like to live life on the edge.

3. Choosie Suzie Hoe

This type of hoe has very short thinking. They like whatever is in front of them. If you put them in a blue dress, blue is their favorite color. If you put them in a red dress the next day, they'll swear that red is their favorite color instead.

If a pimp she's been working for—for let's say one week—sends her off to the hoe stroll to get money in her line of duty, and she's approached by another pimp, best believe that if he gets up in that earpiece good enough, she'll think to herself that he's just got to be a better pimp for her, and choose him. After this routine goes on for a couple of weeks, she'll surely have the reputation of being a Choosie Suzie.

Their loyalty is very limited. They appear to have some sort of fetish or adrenalin rush for seeing what it's like in somebody's program on an often basis.

Somewhere in this type of girl's life, she has had a serious lack of attention that led to some type of physiological effect on her. So when she becomes a participant in the game of pimping and prostitution, and she's approached by several different pimps, besides her own as an invitation to come and work for them, she is overwhelmed with the feeling of being excessively wanted, and she finds it hard to pass up those invitations—which is part of the attention she always lacked.

4. Closet Hoe

A closet hoe is usually one who sees herself living a secret life. Most of the time, she resides in an area that has several other residents. Such as an apartment building or complex. She is more than likely an attractive woman, with an exotic look about herself. Women of this nature are seldom seen, mostly on a coming-or-going basis, and always by herself when she's on the move.

When fellas in the neighborhood attempt to engage in a conversation with her, they are usually turned down with a well-practiced smile, and a charm to go along with it.

This type of woman has her own reasons of why she chooses to keep her discreet line of work away from home, and nobody's business in her local neighborhood. This type of woman is good at mastering the art of keeping people out of her business, and off balanced. But, at the same time, not let anyone feel offended. Yes, she does work on the grounds of prostitution, but she feels that it's better for her if no one is actually aware of where she lives.

5. Complexed Hoe

This characteristic can be found in several different calibers of hoes. Every time they come across someone whom they feel might listen, they're always running a line of bullshit about how them prostituting is the worst thing in the world. They're only doing it 'cause . . .

But they never took five minutes out of their life to see what else they can do instead. They always speak on a change, but it is only done to balance out their complex.

It's just like the persons who claim to have an active faith in a particular religion, but their practice doesn't go any farther than a subconscious thought or small talk.

They do that to soothe and balance out the insecurities of their wrongdoings. Same for the complexed hoe. If anyone ever noticed, where in the world would good people want to be bad, and bad people want to be good? For example, the good youngster out in the suburban upper-class neighborhood watches an R-rated movie about the hood, then all of a sudden, he wants to be a fuckin' gangsta', and take his good living for granted. Knowing he couldn't hang. Then you got a hoe that is, and will always be one. But instead of making the best of it, she's selling herself a dream of one day becoming a Catholic schoolteacher.

People tend to entertain the thought of getting around having to play the hand that was dealt to them.

6.   Conversation Hoe

This kind of hoe is similar to the closet hoe. Only difference is, she openly handles her business. But she has an excuse to try to make herself appear to be something other than a hoe. She has a particular preference of the kind of guys that she feels comfortable turning tricks with. For the ones that she would rather not be bothered with, she'll say something like this: "Shit! I don't sell no pussy. I'll just talk a muthafucka out of his money. I know how to get a dude thinking he might get some pussy, that way he'll keep breaking me off. But ain't nobody getting none of this."

This kind of woman has more landings and take-offs between her legs than LAX Airport, but not if you let her tell it. The black ones who have this type of mentality are usually the ones who refuse to give a black man head, or even allow him to believe that she performs oral copulation. But she'll suck the skin off of a man's dick that's of another ethnicity other than black.

7. Crackhead Hoe

This kind of woman comes from many different walks in life. Depending on whatever kind of situation she may be dealing with currently in her life will make a determination on their person of conduct as a crack user. You got crackhead hoes that live with their children. You have some that are homeless. You have some with style and class, to which crack smoking is only an activity for them. Then you got those who suck dick just to push a pipe with some dude.

Crack can be the cause of a woman's hoeing to be demoted to the lowest form, as I just described. Or it could be the sole purpose in the persistency of her hoeing. Either way, she'll never be able to maintain anything of value for a long period of time. And they won't have very much to show for from their hoeing when it's all said and done.

The only kind of man that a crack-cocaine-using hoe can actually be compatible with is a man who smokes crack just like her, or a pimp who smokes crack as well. As far as a drug-free man, a pimp who has skills in managing a hoe of this caliber would be about the only one who would accept them on a long-term basis.

As far as any other man that is drug free besides a pimp, it'll never work. Besides, a man has to be extremely desperate for companionship if he's willing to accept a crack-cocaine-using woman as his girl. Even if he's a drug dealer who sells what she smokes, he's still going to have to break her off, which will tap into his profit. This is basically a form of indirect tricking, and he's her permanent client.

8. Denial Hoe

This is the hoe that has similar conduct to a prostitute, but she refuses to see herself in that category. The person she usually finds herself exposing her self-proclaimed regard to is mostly a pimp when she is approached by one who has intentions to recruit her. Not necessarily because she's trying to maintain an excuse of why she doesn't want to work for him, but 'cause she honestly feels in her heart that she is better than a prostitute.

She might indulge in things like having sugar daddies, or submit to the approach of strangers who want to have sex with her. But she tells herself, or a particular person that she feels is entitled to an explanation, that she may have dealt with a guy on a sexual basis simply because she was attracted to him to one degree or another. And she'll always accept a "donation," if he chooses to give her one.

That's her nicest interpretation of "turning a trick." Women like this are known to be the ones who have potential in becoming a certified prostitute. But in the meantime, they do indulge in several acts of free fucking. Sooner or later, they do end up getting turned all the rest of the way out by a pimp.

9. Dominatrix Hoe

The regular concept of prostitution is the simplest part of the job for a hoe of this nature. These kinds of women have the stomach to indulge in certain activities with their clients that an ordinary hoe wouldn't. These hoes are the ones who serve the purpose and desire for guys who prefer unusual acts that they have a certain fetish for. Such as pain being applied to them in one form or another by a woman. Being recessive to the woman who is serving him with a strap-on dildo (which is definitely homosexual tendencies). Preferring a woman to discharge her urine or feces onto him and several other obscene acts.

Women who are specifically the ones for this job are not usually found on the hoe stroll, or a product of a pimp. They are usually found through some kind of service upon someone's request. Not to say that an ordinary prostitute hasn't experienced a date with a man who preferred an obscene act that they catered to. But for the most part, this has got to be the most obscene form of prostitution.

10. Dope fiend / Junkie Hoe

There are different levels of classifications for a heroin-addict hoe. Depending on how severe the habit is or how they use the drug, depends a lot on their willingness or performance as a prostitute. Women who mainline heroin (inject intravenously) and have been doing it for a long time, are known for having scars and tracks on multiple places on their bodies, including their legs.

They may also have scars from abscesses. These scars usually result in hoes wearing full-length pants to cover them while she's working. Since mainlining gives heroin the fullest effect, women waste a lot of time that could be put into their hoeing by nodding off and getting lazy. Also, it sometimes takes them awhile to successfully find a vein to shoot up in. For the ones who snort it, or use the "chasing the dragon method" (smoking it), it doesn't have any effect on their external appearance, and their routine dosages are not as time consuming.

Futhermore, it has less of an effect on their conduct compared to a mainliner, which enables them to be a bit more focused in their line of duty. Their conduct of loyalty and ethics are similar to those of a crack-cocaine user. And a high percentage of junkie hoes use crack as well.

As I described with the crackhead hoe, the only kind of man that a junkie can have is a junkie like herself—a junkie pimp or a sober pimp. They are at their most vulnerable state when they are dope sick. They will indulge in any type of sex act, as long as it's enough to overcome their sickness. Their mood swings are severe, and their thoughts are disorientated, unless they have a man to stabilize them.

11. Drag Queen Hoe

This breed of prostitutes consists of men who dress up as women. They are either transvestites (men who dress as women and have female characteristics due to the use of hormone pills) or transsexuals (men who had an operational sex change).

Either way, they are gay men who portray themselves to be women that are prostitutes. Most major cities that have hoe strolls that serve the purpose for pimps and their prostitutes also have a particular hoe stroll for drag queens. For the most part, the drag queens are out there working with the intention to deceive tricks and potential johns that they're women—and most of the time, it works.

But then on the other hand, there are a large number of tricks that know that this breed of prostitutes consists of men, and that is what they are particularly looking for. Sometimes when times get hard for drag queens on their particular track, they'll sneak their way onto a track where there are real female prostitutes, and try their luck there.

12. Fun-time Hoe

This type of bitch ought to be ashamed of herself. She's very lucky to have the word *hoe* included in her description to any extent. She will indulge in all types of promiscuous sex acts just to have something to do. She doesn't care much about receiving benefits for her services. If she does, she does. If she don't, she don't!

She gives pussy on credit, and even sometimes on layaway. And there are even a few of them who feel that prostitution is degrading. They'll say things like, "I'm not going to sell my body. If I like a guy, I'll give it to him because I like him. Not because he's paying me for it."

What is so nerve-wracking is the number of guys she calls herself "liking," that she's doing all of this free fucking with? If she were to have gotten paid $50 for every guy that she had sex with, her yearly salary would be running neck and neck with the president's. The only productive service that this hoe serves is catering to a man's ego that he got some free pussy!

13. Immigrant Hoe

These women are strictly foreigners who have agreed to allow themselves to be exploited on the basis of remaining in the United States. Or was somehow lead to believe that they can possibly become citizens through real or falsified documents, in exchange for their services as a prostitute.

They are usually managed by the fellas who contributed to them illegally entering the country, or by the person they were bought by. For most of them, whorehouses serve as their base. Then again, you have a lot who may be assigned to work a designated area as a street prostitute.

They work and live under totally different guidelines than a prostitute who works for a general black pimp. However, there are certain rules that are laid out for them to abide by from the person who is in charge of them. Things like how to respond to someone who tries to encourage them to work for him instead. (Mostly a black guy.) And also, what chances they are taking if they choose to run off and disregard their assigned program.

The fact of how they will be deported by INS is one thing that they are constantly made aware of to make them think twice about running off, or doing something other than what they're told.

14. Lesbian Hoe

These breeds of women do not like men. The thought of them ever being with a pimp is a thought they don't entertain. A man to them is nothing more than an object to serve their financial needs.

The only person that they will allow themselves to serve as a significant other to is indeed another woman. To them, sex with men is as superficial as it gets. Some of these women are drug addicts, and some of them aren't. But all of them report home to a woman when it's all said and done. For the ones who don't have a woman, they'll still be within arm's reach of one whom they prefer to cater to their sexual desires.

Not to say that any of them haven't ever been with a pimp somewhere in their past, let alone a man. But something led up to them feeling comfortable with a woman instead. These women are very crafty, conniving, and influential. They pass up no opportunity when they see vulnerability in a pimp's woman. A lot of them think that any woman with a pimp is stupid, or doesn't know any better. And they themselves feel that they can be a pimp.

15. Play a Pimp Hoe

There is no other category to put this hoe in other than an asshole! She gets a kick out of having a pimp expect a productive performance from her, and then not live up to her expectations.

She is in denial of the concept of pimping and feels that he is no exception from getting played as she does all other men. This type of bitch has a countless number of pimps under her belt that she has agreed upon intention to give his program an honest effort. And when the time came to let her actions show, she either used the pimp for means of transportation, or simply chose to keep it moving in the opposite direction when she hopped in a car with a trick she turned.

What makes her naughty little motive all the way intentional is she'll try her best to convince the pimp that she'll be able to perform just as good, if not "better" than whatever other hoes used for comparison. Then try her luck with seeing how far the pimp will go as far as investing in her.

Things like a new outfit, makeup, shoes, and with hoes that get high-on drugs. Then without any remorse, she'll split the first opportunity she gets. What makes it even worse, if the pimp is seasoned or experienced, he'll let her know that he's aware of any negative, or transgressive thoughts that might cross her mind, giving her a hint to throw her hand in right there if she's bullshitting.

Does she take heed to that? No! She follows all the way through with her anticipated, deceiving thoughts.

16. Massage Parlor Hoe

These women are the ones who work in a massage parlor and give their services specifically to clients who know what they're there for. Although the acts of prostitution is kept somewhat low-key, especially for someone who is square to what else goes on inside of the parlor besides massages, there is still heavy prostitution going on.

The massage parlors that a lot of clients are familiar with have Asian women who work inside of them. Although this activity is being in a public place of business, it is still illegal just like any other source of nontax-paying prostitution.

As far as Asian women who work inside of them, their business acquaintances as far as financial management, or assistance, is usually kept within their own kind of people.

17. Police Hoe

The title speaks for itself. This woman is a police officer who imposes herself to be a prostitute in an undercover capacity. Her goal is to bust pimps and potential tricks. They use several different techniques, such as . . .

Indulging with other prostitutes (real ones) on the basis of conversations with them to find out who their pimps are. Making themselves present in an area where pimps are known to be at, either in crowds or driving around. And also busting tricks for soliciting to a prostitute.

The way they get pimps is by making their self-visible to whichever one(s) they know are going to approach them. Knowing that by imposing themselves as a prostitute, it'll never fail. Once they are approached by a pimp who is in hot pursuit of a new prostitute, she'll make herself appear to be vulnerable and up for grabs, then indulge in a conversation with him until he gives her a proposition to work for him.

Once that part of the conversation takes place, a crime will be considered committed and her police buddies that are in the cuts, assisting her in their "sting," will move in for the bust.

18. Porno Industry Hoe

These types of hoes are safe from the law. In addition to that, they are taxpayers. But they're still hoes! Women have their reasons of wanting to become involved in the porno industry.

Some were already sexually promiscuous, and beautiful. So they combined their awareness of both of their advantages, and used them to get paid, and become somewhat famous. Others already had a foot in the door by being a part of some kind of sexual service. And others were encouraged to be exploited in this manner by someone they knew or met.

Either way, it is the most publicized form of prostitution. It is not something that's done in a somewhat "discreet" manner, with the exception of leaving the audience, or would-be audience with the choice to entertain that kind of material, or not.

Here's the difference between the porno industry hoes and street-walking prostitutes: Porno stars are not only making a living from having sex, they are entertaining as well (during their sexual performances). To where a streetwalking hoe is simply getting paid for her sexual services alone.

As far as a porno industry hoe's personal life, it may vary—just like any other woman's life.

19. Religious Hoe

These particular women are indeed a rare breed. Not everybody will be able to say that they've ever encountered one. But they do exist!

A religious hoe is a woman who was once an active prostitute, but now she sees herself as one who made a transitional change in her life and has became familiar with God. (The Christian God.)

She is only as retired as she considers herself. This hypocritical hoe uses the Word of God to try to get familiar with pimps on a religious basis. They usually have a feature or two about themselves that catches a pimp's attention if he lets it. For the pimps that allow this kind of woman to develop the acquaintance with them that she wants, they usually find themselves becoming as disappointed with her, to the same degree as a hoe that ran off on them.

What their purpose is for becoming the way they are is unknown. They live what may be described as a double life. They are religious in front of the people who they want to know them as that. Then they live their discreet life with the ones they feel it applies to. It is highly possibly that this kind of woman has multiple personalities.

20. Renegade Hoe

A renegade hoe is a hoe without a pimp under certain circumstances. First and foremost, it is true indeed that every hoe doesn't have a pimp, and furthermore, there are women who will not allow themselves to be pimped. But what classifies a hoe as a renegade is the fact of how this type of woman is one who, at one time or another, did have a pimp. But for one reason or another, that is no longer the case.

What she does is take the specific knowledge of techniques and conduct that she was accustomed to when she worked for a pimp, then use that in her line of duty on mainline hoe strolls that are stomping grounds for prostitutes that work for pimps.

Her conduct will leave a pimp, who is trying to approach her, under the impression that she might work for somebody. Not that hoe strolls are necessarily territorial, but any pimp who discovers such woman to be a renegade would take offence to her presence.

She is basically making an indirect statement that she can gain the financial benefits from such hoe stroll in the same exact matter as a hoe with a pimp—only she doesn't have one, by choice. She is also a bad influence on pimp's woman. It would be better for a drug addict hoe to pop up on a hoe stroll during its prime moments, 'cause her presence would not be taken as offensively as a renegade's. The drug addict hoe is putting forth effort to support her habit. The renegade hoe is basically saying, "Fuck pimps."

21. Retired Hoe

This is a woman who came to a conclusion that she's done all of the prostitution that she's going to do. There are several different scenarios that can lead up to a woman making such rare decision. While there's a small number of those who chose not to deal with prostitution-related activities anymore, there's even a smaller number of women that choose not to even be sexually promiscuous anymore as well.

A woman that has ever carried out the career as a prostitute in her life will always have a physiological effect on them afterwards. She might scorn certain sex acts with her mate—such as oral sex or anal sex, or whatever else—'cause it might remind her of a regretful era of her life.

Then there are hoes, on the other hand, who are as freaky as can be, and opened to any sexual activity with their mate. They appreciate indulging in these activities with somebody that's their man, or they're honestly attracted to, as opposed to the tricks and clients that they did not genuinely desire.

Some women have reason of wanting to retire prostituting on a long-term basis, while others stopped not too much longer after they got a foot in the door. They could've had a bad experience. Or the person who talked them into giving it a try led them to a disappointment.

22. Set-up Hoe

This hoe gets more of a kick out of contributing to somebody getting robbed than she does selling pussy. Some might be prostitutes, and others may be inactive prostitutes, while there's some who may not have ever prostituted a day in their life.

But they all have experience in setting somebody up to be robbed by some guy(s). It may be a pimp who is somebody's target, and the fellas who intend on robbing him probably believes that the best way to catch him slipping is by sending a bitch at him.

So the bitch may cross his path as an imposter presenting herself as one who's taking interest in working for him. Once her part is successfully done, the fellas will move in for the jack.

Another method that set-up hoes use is robbing tricks. They'll lure a potential john off to a designated area where the fellas may be waiting to jump out and ambush him. The women who indulge in this type of activity mostly come out of a ghetto neighborhood where this kind of activity is in their nature. They may be with a certain guy who doesn't want them to sell pussy, so he'll turn her into this kind of woman instead. Or she may be a hoe who is with a pimp that still has gangster tendencies in him, and living off of his woman's earnings from her prostituting may not be accumulating enough money to satisfy him. So he's not going to hesitate to go for a bonus from time to time.

23) Streetwalker Hoe

A streetwalker hoe is the most common form of prostitute, as the world knows it. When all else fails for a woman, as far as trying to get into some kind of service, instead of making a public appearance with her trade, the streets will never let her down—no matter how she looks. All a woman needs to sell pussy are two legs, a slit, a mouth to please and negotiate with.

Somebody is going to come out of their pockets, 'cause all pussy sells! Maybe not at the same pace, but somebody will like what they see. Depending on what town or city a woman is in will determine which conducts and methods she will use while she's working those particular streets. Also, the time of day or night might require different methods as well.

A seasoned hoe will break luck at any given moment it's presented to her, whether she's on her scheduled shift or not. The only time she would pass up a legitimate date is if it would be entirely interrupting to an agenda she already has, or if she's en route to somewhere she has to be. In some cases, the woman may pass up a date 'cause they believe that the law is somewhere nearby, waiting to intervene.

Woman who use the streetwalking alternative must develop a strong source of intelligence in this particular department, due to the dangers and risks that come along with it. For the hoes that have pimps, the pimp should be able to assist them with the proper instructions and guidance necessary, in order for the streets to be a productive alternative.

24. Strip Club Hoe

Women who work in strip clubs come from different walks of life. Some do that on the side from a totally different occupation, and others do it by means of financial support.

But whatever the reason is, they're still one step away from being a prostitute. There is not much of a difference in morality when it comes to a woman who brandishes her naked body and allows her private parts to be felt on while she's sitting on some guys lap while his dick is rock hard than a prostitute who just follows all the way through with sex.

Some women go into a strip club to work, and can never see themselves actually having "sex" for money. But a lot of different things come to mind when one of those clients in the strip club whispers in that bitche's ear that he'll give her $500 or even $1500 if she gives him a call when she gets off of work, and schedule a date.

There are some women who work in strip clubs that build a clientele of those kinds of guys. Then there are some that just haven't come around yet. In a strip club, a woman is either a "safe hoe" or a "potential hoe."

25. Thieving Hoe

All hoes have thieving characteristics in them. If a hoe catches a trick slipping 'cause he's drunk, sober, or stupid, she's going to get him. It's part of her job. But the ones who live up to this title are the ones who specialize in stealing every chance they get.

They are known to make hoe strolls hot, in terms of causing one of their victims to call the police on them, behind the hoe jumping out of a trick's car with his wallet, cell phone, or whatever the hell else. In some situations, this shit causes them to become a victim themselves.

The difference between a thieving hoe and a regular hoe stealing from a trick is, the thieving hoe is petty and carefree. She is a kleptomaniac. She will take a guy by the hand in the act if finessing, and try to slip a ring off his finger during the departure of their hands.

She will give a man a hug in the same manner, and put forth effort to dip in his pockets in hopes of pulling out what she is blindly fishing for. Some even have the heart to persist once they've been caught. And some don't even mind stealing from their own pimp in the process of her unexpected departure.

26. Welfare Hoe

A welfare hoe isn't in the category of a prostitute. She has a little twist to her program. The only sex she has to have to get money from the welfare department is the sex that gets her pregnant.

A lot of women become a welfare hoe unconsciously. All they know is that they're already accustomed to receiving a certain amount of money from welfare for however many children they have. So another child that she gives birth to means more money every month when she gets her check.

Then you have those, mostly foreigners, who purposely have multiple babies for the sole purpose of receiving a fat check. Anyone who has lived in some kind of neighborhood that was below middle class has seen a house, or an apartment, that was occupied by several children, adolescents, and babies. It's no accident!

27. Whorehouse Hoe

Women work in whorehouses under different circumstances. It all depends on what kind of whorehouse they're affiliated with. The proper term for a whorehouse is a brothel, and they have them all over the world. As far as the ones that are legal, the women who work in them are usually checked frequently for any STDs. They usually deal with the clients right there in the house.

As far as the privately ran, or should I say tax-free whorehouses, there are several different programs that can be used to operate each one individually. There are whorehouses in other countries that have women working in them on the verge of slavery. Then you got some here in the United States that have a house full of women that work on the basis of the immigrant hoe (which I described in no. 13).

Then you might have a pimp who sets up something close to a whorehouse for his girls by using a garage, backhouse, hotel or motel room, or any other form of an alternative residence.

28. Workplace Hoe

These particular hoes think they're slick. They believe that they're so far out of the category of a prostitute, or anything in regards to one, that you couldn't pay them to entertain the thought of their name being in the same sentence with the word *hoe*. These women have jobs in an industrial environment that has a lot of coworkers—including males.

What these certain women do, only for the purpose to get money, is allow their acts of prostitution to be applied to no one other than their male coworkers. Yes! She is the hot piece of ass at the job that all the fellas know about.

They all know that they can be well taken care of by her if they break her off a piece of that paycheck every two weeks. She works there as well. And she's been known to get away with certain things that everybody can't. Sometimes, she may even get a position that she would rather prefer, before others whose been there longer than her. Why? 'Cause that's the power that pussy has. Additionally, this kind of woman—whether consciously, subconsciously, or unconsciously—is hoeing in one of the safest forms there is.

Bonus Hoe: The Punk Bitch

This hoe is the hoe that puts a pimp in jail, and has no remorse about doing so. There are several situations occuring when a pimp may go to jail or prison over a hoe. It could have started out as something unintentional, such as a pimp sweating a hoe in an effort to recruit her. The police may have observed this activity taking place, and chose to intervene.

Instead of the hoe accepting the matter as one of the many natural occurrences in her line of duty, her short thinking will allow her to believe that if she cooperates with the police once they've intervened, it would be best for the pimp to go to jail. That way, they figure they won't be sweated by that particular pimp anymore.

Another spur-of-the-moment occurrence where a pimp goes to jail 'cause of a hoe unintentionally is when there's domestic violence activity going on in a household. Let's say, a hotel-motel room or an apartment complex, and the pimp is in the process of disciplining one of his employees. When a neighbor happens to hear the commotion, he or she decides to call the police. Now when the police shows up, instead of the bitch telling them that they got the wrong residence, she dry-snitches on her pimp by making apparent signs in front of them that she's just been through an episode of domestic violence.

Now here's an example of an unanticipated one, but when the moment presents itself, it becomes intentional. When a hooker is arrested for prostitution, she shows the police signs of weakness as a result of being arrested. If the hoe doesn't volunteer an offer, the police will move in on the weakness she's showing and ask her what she's willing to give up in exchange for her arrest being disregarded. (Not a blow job.)

Hoes like this, regardless if they've been schooled properly by their pimps on how to go about situations such as this, the bitch will still tell the police whom she works for and how they can find him, in order not to be arrested for prostitution. Shit, in some cases the bitch will all out assist the police with the sting.

Now what's really fucked up about some of these scenarios and any that may be similar to them is, this woman is not thinking for the future well-being of the man that she's putting in jail. Regardless of what the situation is, she will have an opportunity, when the police have her to herself, to tell them all that needs to be said in order for the police not to entertain the thought of arresting the pimp.

But in this case, she does the total opposite. There has been a situation where a hoe has assisted the police in developing a nasty police report against her pimp at the least, and took it all the way to the witness stand to testify against him at the most. Her motive may not have started off being that bad at first, but when a pimp is involved, the police use several interrogating techniques to make her turn against him.

They brainwash her into thinking that any man that has her working the streets is an asshole, and wouldn't give two fucks if she lives or dies. The hoe falls victim to one of her own weak characteristics—agreeing with whatever is in front of her! Her pimp, in her presence, is her lord and savior, the best thing that ever happened to her; then when the police are in her presence and they brainwash her with their psychological techniques, her pimp becomes the devil himself.

What's sad about the situation is, once this man is sent off to prison because of her, she'll be doing the exact same thing. If not on her own basis, then on another pimp's basis. Her putting that man in jail was only a result of her vulnerability—not a step toward changing her life!

So while the pimp is making collect phone calls, instead of using a cell phone; while being entertained by *Black Video Illustrated, Buttman,* and *Hustler* magazines, a.k.a. paper pussy, instead of a real woman in the flesh; while eating Top Ramen soups as a delicacy, instead of going to a restaurant of his choice; and while months or years are being taken away from his life—the time that he will never be able to get back, the day he got arrested is only past tense to the hoe that was responsible for it.

Life will move on for her, and that superficial incident to her will be the last thing on her mind while she's doing what she does. To make it even worse, if she's currently with another pimp after that kind of incident has occurred, and he is notified by other players in the game that he has a hoe with a reputation for putting pimps in the jailhouse, that information will be of no importance to him. Why? 'Cause if she's productive to his program, he will not let her irrelevant history affect that. Furthermore, he will have faith and confidence in his own pimpin' not to allow himself to experience that type of misfortune with that particular hoe.

This kind of hoe may seem to be getting away with the misfortune that she consciencelessly, subconsciously, or unconsciously inflicted on some pimpin'. But where her heart is at—as far as willingly, or unwillingly, cracking under pressure with the law—she will not last that long as a participant in a street game, before she experiences a great misfortune of her own.

Stereotypes, Opinions, and Myths

Prostitutes! Can't live with them, can't live without them, can't live without having something to say about them either! They may not be as controversial as pimps, but they do bring reason for people to form an opinion about them when they can't have it their way with a hoe.

Even other females who think they're better than a prostitute come up with something to say. They may not like the fact that there's a certain attractive prostitute in the same vicinity where her man is. So she'll spread a rumor that the hoe has AIDS or HIV.

It might be a trick that has dealt with a prostitute on a number of occasions; and upon his own choice, he decided to try to see the prostitute as more of a "woman" figure instead of the hoe she is, and develop feelings for her. When reality sets in on him that she isn't *his* woman but "the world's" woman when they can afford her, his soul becomes disturbed, and he can't handle it.

He might commence to a childlike act, such as starting rumors about her in hopes of bringing inconvenience to her everyday life. He'll say things about her being a thief who she lied on and put in jail for rape. She done gave "whomever" STD and they ended up taking antibiotics. And a whole lot of other silly shit.

Sometimes, a hoe brings this type of nonsense on herself without even realizing it. Her finessing skills that she portrays to her tricks are sometimes a little too over the top. He's falling in love with her, and she's setting herself up for failure. And the aforementioned actions that he'll carry out are the "least" results.

Set aside from people's personal encounters with prostitutes, you got the stereotypes about them as well. It has been said that "all hoes do something" in terms of drugs. But that isn't true. They believe that a woman has to have a mind-altering stimulant in order for them to accept what they do, but at the same time, be in a different mind frame. Bullshit!

Woman that are prostitutes that have habits, whether they came into the game with them, or picked them up along the way, their drug addiction is irrelevant. A sober hoe is one who doesn't exceed beyond these substances: cigarettes, coffee, marijuana, and occasionally alcohol. Why would that categorize her as a sober individual? Well, for one, with the exception of cigarettes, none of these substances require an excessive or consistent use. Second of all, none of them are a $50 and up a day habit.

As far as alcohol, some women use it more or less than others. While some abuse it, some occasionally use it! But for the most part, those minor substances that have little effect on one's conduct and financial budget should not be the least reason to classify all Ladies of Leisure as having a habit. If that were the case, it would equal to saying, "All people living who are the age of thirteen (13) and up have some kind of habit."

In other words, it is a myth that is more applicable to the world, not just hoes. Then there *are* hoes that have a drug addiction that makes them stand out as an all out addict. Okay. Big deal! It is what it is with them. Some smoke crack. Some shoot cocaine. Some sniff cocaine. Some use heroin in one form or another. Some use methamphetimine in one form or another. Some abuse the shit out of alcohol. But you got people from all walks of life that do those same drugs as well.

Another thing that people tend to stereotype about hoes is that "they'll do anything" as far as not having a limit to the sexual activities that they'll indulge in, in their line of duty. Each hooker has her own limitation with her dos and don'ts. You got the kinds who are complexes about performing fellatio—more commonly known as giving head.

It's possible that they may have been abused as a child, and oral sex is something they're disturbed by. Then there's some that feel like giving a man some head is spoiling him and stroking his ego to the extent where she doesn't feel it deserves to be stroked. Then you got some who are very selective of who they'll give head to. If it's an everyday face and the hoe doesn't particularly like the guy, she'll leave him with the impression that she doesn't suck dick. She'll feel more comfortable dealing with people that she doesn't have to deal with on an everyday basis when it comes to that.

That way, they won't be around her to verify her as a liar. Then there are those who simply have mood swings. One day, they'll be up to do whatever with whomever. The next day, they done came up with some kind of moral. (Yeah right!)

On a whole other note, you got some hoes that prefer to do nothing more than suck dick. Some women who are in the business of prostitution have insecurity about the way that their vagina can become stretched out of shape in a form that they wouldn't feel comfortable with. Others feel that their pussy is sacred and don't like just anybody taking control of them physically in that manner. They would rather run the show, give the guy a blow job, and go on about her way.

Then there are some (the majority) who look at the concept of prostitution in the manner of being paid for making the man feel good by whatever common activities necessary. Some hoes don't take any chances when performing oral sex without a condom being worn on the guy's penis. They believe that if they don't allow the man to ejaculate in their mouth, they'll be free from the possibility of contracting diseases. Then you got those who don't bother to use condoms for such activity 'cause they have a particular fetish for the taste of cum in their mouth.

Then you got your hoes that exist who won't even touch a man's dick without a condom being placed on it first. Some are very cautious of catching any STDs. Others may have a man at home of some sort a pimp, a boyfriend, a sugar daddy, or even young children. They would see it as disrespectful to return to the presence of them in their household after their mouth has made excessive direct contact with several penises.

And furthermore, any hoe with common sense usually uses protection during standard sex with a stranger in their line of duty. You got some that will not allow a trick that they don't know give it to them up the ass, regardless if he's willing to wear a condom. They may feel that it isn't a trick's position or place to receive that much gratification from that particular sex act, when he'll just settle for the basics and she'll still walk off with the same amount of money.

Then she might indulge with somebody who's breaking her off money, and she's physically attracted to him to whatever extent, and allows him to give it to her up the ass 'cause it's catering to her sexual desire, along with her financial needs.

So there you have it. Some hoes do this; some hoes do not do that!

But the moral of the topic is this: the same extent that prostitutes go through, as far as their limitations, is the same for just about any other woman who is sexually active. Unless she's married, and sexually moralistic to her husband.

Another stereotype about a hooker is, "they enjoy what they do." Once again, that is a myth that applies to hoes individually, not as a whole. There are some who indeed like being a prostitute, and everything that comes along with it, especially sex! There are many that will flat out admit that they enjoy "sucking dick." And they'll boldly accept their job for what it is. They'll tell somebody in a heartbeat that they "enjoy entertaining men by any means necessary." There is no complex or insecurities about them.

Then, on the other hand, there are hoes that feel guilty about being a prostitute. The reason that they remain as one is their self-esteem has always been too low for them to try to resort to something else. Subconsciously, they feel that their hand calls for something else, but they never had a push of impulsive motivation in another regards.

They try to view every nonbeneficial occurrence in their line of duty as something that makes them hate their position just that much more. They have a weak will, and they resort to the easiest thing they can—look pretty, let herself be seen and desired, and remain open game for any man interested who has some money.

While some people think that *all* hoes enjoy being a prostitute and think that it's all uphill for them, there's some hoes who see the overall concept as being similar to a street dealer who sells drugs. The dealer may be outside in all sorts of weather conditions.

He constantly encounters chances of selling to an undercover. Being or attempted to be robbed. Snitched on by an unknown source. Constantly dealing with people who make his stomach churn. People always trying to be slick and come out on top of the deal. People always approaching him on the grounds of trying to get something on credit, or in advance. People who do not take care of their hygiene and have an offensive odor when they approach him to purchase something. Dealing with people who are not always in their right frame of mind, and acting a damn fool in his presence.

These are the things that they have to deal with every time they step outside to hustle. If they took the time to sit back and think about all the things they don't like about their job, all the above-mentioned risks and occurrences would come to mind. Those incidents right there can actually cause them to believe that they hate the game. But still and all, there are many who don't bother to change their occupation, or attempt to advance their level of the game. Why? Because what they've been doing is easy money for them, and it gets them by.

Especially when they have their good moments. Like when they flip their whole amount that they just bought in the blink of an eye, and make more than their expected quota. It's things like that in their line of business that makes them feel that all the hardship is worth it.

Same concept goes for the prostitute. Her judgment of how she feels about the game goes up and down with the good and bad occurrences in her life. It is only common sense that a hoe doesn't like the inconvenient occurrences that goes on, such as having to stand the smell of a trick's unwashed crotch area when she unzips his pants to give him a blow job.

Having to convince a trick to wear a condom, even if it's only for oral sex. Getting inside of a car with an idiot who's talking about some dumb-assed ten- or fifteen-dollar shit. Tricks not wanting to let her out of the car. Tricks who take, or attempt to take, the money back. Party people and assholes that like to harass hookers by grabbing their ass and hollering bullshit out of the window. And even sometimes running them over while they're in the middle of the street.

Not wanting to be bothered by certain tricks who don't know how to take no for an answer, and persist to the point where it becomes annoying or agitating. Why does a hoe put up with this? Well, just like the street hustler, she will have a long line of beneficial experiences to go along with the nonbeneficial ones.

There will be plenty of times where she will encounter a trick who she is dating for the first time, and he'll give her a few hundred dollars after it took him only three minutes to bust a nutt. Then he gets her phone number, and becomes one of her regular clients. There will be days, and nights, where she will make well over her expected quota, and not have any problems breaking luck, or have run-ins with the law. Moments like those are the ones that will cause her to see the game as being worth it, and her esteem will be high.

Any myth, figure of speech, or stereotype that someone places on a hoe is usually one that can be used to stereotype women as a whole. It's just the outlook that people have on prostitutes that causes their negative focus to be directed toward a prostitute when they want to imply a stereotype.

When it's a man that has a certain hoe's name all up in his mouth, he'll usually place the overall stereotypes of hookers on her. His gossip is so superficial; all it would take for him to disregard anything he said about her would be a blow job, or a shot of pussy.

One of the most things that are said about a hoe that has a pimp is that "she's stupid for having one." Well, excuse the hell out of her for having some kind of man that she can keep it real with. How about every other female who has a different occupation, being the only ones to have someone to call their significant other, while a prostitute only deals with the kind of men that I described earlier (tricks) who either piss these women off while they're trying to make a living, or are extremely humble to women with absolutely no charisma to put an authentic smile on their face.

Yes, there are hoes with pimps, and they do give them the money that they make. Why not? In simplified terms, a hoe is a pimp's woman. And any man who shares his woman with another man should receive financial benefits for it.

People also tend to stereotype hoes according to their ethnicity. You got your stereotypes about your black hoes. Your white hoes. Your light-skinned mixed hoes. And your Hispanic hoes. Let's go over the matter of the black hoes first. We hear it all the time: "Black bitches got a fuckin attitude. That's why I don't fuck with them." And a whole lot of other shit that's generally said. You got pimps who have a certain outlook on black hoes. You got squares that have a certain outlook on them. There are even tricks who have a certain outlook on them. There are several pimps who don't accept black women in their stable of prostitutes, due to past experiences with them. There may have been a time earlier in their career where they evaluated all of the type of women which works best for him, and black hoes ended up being the ones he would rather not prefer. It may have been because of the defiance he saw in them. Or a ghetto mentality that he would rather not deal with. Or several other things that lead up to his conclusion.

However, his perspective may be different from that of other pimps. There are black hoes that have served a pimp the purpose of his existence better than a hoe of any other nationality. You got some tricks who have had a runaround experience with black women, to where when they're looking for a hooker to pick up, they might accept anything but a black one. In their past experience with a black hoe, they may have went through the "fake blowjob" incident. That's where a hoe is giving a trick a hand job, but trying to fool him that her mouth is really on his penis. For whatever the hell her reason is for wanting to do that, who knows! It could have been a lack of submissiveness, or an unreasonable price. All the trick knows is that his encounters with black hoes were regretful, and black women are not of his preference.

Statistic wise, there is a larger percentage of black hoes that is obstinate than those who aren't. That's why they have the stereotype that they do. Everyone—pimps, tricks, and whoever else—may not have come across a submissive black hoe before they came to the conclusion of not even wanting to be bothered with them. There are plenty of black hoes that are submissive, loyal, honorable, and obedient to their program and pimp. And furthermore, there are also black hoes that are what we consider "freaks" and are sexually opened for most activities necessary in their line of duty. These are the black hoes that count in the game.

Then you got your all-American white girls. Hitler's finest. The ones that everybody watched on their television set growing up. The ones that caused a lot of guys to think to themselves, "How can I ever get a girlfriend like that?" The ones who contributed to *Playboy* being what it is today.

The stereotypes that people have on white hoes are totally different than those of a black hoe. You'll hear things like, "White hoes are very submissive." "White women are freaks who'll do anything sexually. They'll lick your asshole. Swallow your nutt. Take it up the ass. Suck ten dicks back to back." And a whole lot of other things.

Sure there are white women who do all of that. They got that reputation from the majority of them being sexually open. But at the same time, there are women of all races who are sexually open on an equal basis. But as the old saying has it, "Majority rules," and the majority of guys who have encountered with white hoes recalled enjoying them.

But as a whole—no! White hoes are not *all* submissive and freaky. Some, after a while, gain the mannerism of a black hoe. (The black hoe that turns people away from her.) And they piss people off. A lot of them are vulnerable to the curiosity of experimenting different kinds of drugs, and many do eventually become full-fledged addicts. Once they've become addicts, their conduct will include a lot of domineering and malicious acts. Everything that somebody once thought that they liked about a white hoe will definitely be disregarded with one of this nature. They always try to be slick. Lying and fabricating a story becomes a second nature to them. And their obedience runs about as far as a mouse when someone tells it not to "bother a piece of cheese" after they left it with him.

However, white women in general were raised to have a totally different train of thought, as opposed to a black woman. A lot of pimps have had more successful results from white women 'cause they come equipped with a certain chemistry that works perfectly for a white woman. In addition, white women had a different upbringing than black women.

Most of them grew up in the house with both their mother and father. They became accustomed to accepting authority from a male figure at an early age. So the concept of having a pimp once they become an age where they're sexually promiscuous is not something that's hard for them to see the logic in. They don't mind being submissive to a daddy figure. As far as their sexual conduct is concerned, they're not complexes to where giving a man some head or indulging in anal sex are degrading to them.

As far as black women, most who become prostitutes grew up in an inner-city environment, where a large percentage of black youths didn't have both parents in their household, especially the father. So from the beginning of her life cycle, she was not used to being submissive to a male figure. With their sexual conduct, a lot of them are "complexed" and/or very selective to certain sex acts. Giving a blow job or taking a dick up their butthole is something that a lot of them do see as degrading—whether they follow through with it or not.

The environments that they grew up in had always allowed those activities to appear degrading. They may have had brothers or homies with the "hustler" or "gangsta" mentality. That's why, if a black hoe in general decides to submit to oral or anal sex, they'll rather deal with someone who is the total opposite from the fellas she grew up around—like a square white or a square Hispanic guy. That way, they won't feel that they're being looked down upon the way they're familiar with the average black man from the "hood" looking down on women who "sucked their dick last night," or "let a nigga fuck her in the ass."

So that's where the difference comes from in the nature of a black hoe's sexual conduct, as opposed to a white hoe's. The original environments. This isn't the same for all situations. But since people form an opinion about matters that they've seen the majority of, these are the general scenarios in a common aspect, in response to a common outlook.

Hispanic women also play a large role in the prostitution trade. Depending on what section of the country we're talking about determines what breed of Hispanic women are mostly found there. In the western section, midwestern section, and a large portion of southern states, there are several Hispanic women who make up the ethnicities of Mexican, El Salvadorian, Peruvian, Columbian, Honduran, Nicaraguan, Ecuadorian, and Panamanian.

On the East Coast, from Maine to Florida and everything in between (and/or nearby), you'll find the Hispanic population to be made up of mostly Caribbean Hispanics such as Puerto Rican, Dominican, and Cuban. (Any Hispanic group left out probably serves a small portion of the U.S. population.)

Most people have always perceived Hispanic women to be ones who posses a great deal of loyalty. Not being ones to do a lot of talking back. And not have any problem being totally submissive to their man. As far as the ones who are Americanized, their conduct usually becomes equivalent to white drug addict hoes, once they're hardcore substance abusers.

The ones who aren't drug addicts that are Americanized usually gain certain characteristics, and mannerism that are similar to those of a black woman's. Especially those who are with a pimp. Besides, they're under a black man who does black things. Flips through black magazines. Listens to black music. And most of all, indulges in a black man's line of business.

However, the loyal ethics that they are inherited with are still with them. Hispanic women usually come out of a large family with the majority of their family members present. They grew up seeing sex as a natural part of life. Once they're sexually active, activities like giving head are not at all looked at as degrading, 'cause the men who were in their original environment were not immature about the matter of women performing oral copulation. Therefore, they don't have any complexities about sex.

In some cases with those who become familiar with prostitution, they distance themselves from their families. Not too many Hispanic families will accept the knowledge of their sister, daughter, granddaughter—or whatever the relationship is to her—becoming a prostitute to whatever degree.

By the hoe already knowing that they would probably disown her for this, she respectfully keeps it as far away from their knowledge as possible. Unless she comes from a particular family that lives in an underworld setting of some type, they really wouldn't be happy to know if she also had a black pimp. A lot of Hispanics (besides the ones from the Caribbean islands) are typically not in favor of a woman in their family having a black man—let alone a pimp.

As far as Oriental women, they too have a reputation for being humble and submissive. Any pimp who includes at least one of them in his stable is definitely a fortunate individual. Every man enjoys the thought of having sex with a woman of a particular ethnicity that he doesn't encounter with on an often basis. And an Oriental woman is right up a guy's alley who's looking for a prostitute.

They have no problem breaking luck. That goes into the stereotype of which hoe of a certain nationality can make the most money. First of all, Oriental women—as rare as the opportunity ever presents itself in many men's lifetime to ever have sex with one—will make a lot of money and not have a hard time catching clients, or building a clientele of high-paying clients. As long as she's attractive. Other than that, it all depends on what the trick is looking for.

A very popular stereotype is, "White hoes make the most money"! But that's not necessarily true. What is true is that a white hoe is the easiest to approach. Men of all different ethnicities, whether they speak English or not, for some reason are bold with their approach toward a white hoe. In some cases, it's 'cause he may feel that his communication with her may be simple and does not require that much hassle.

As far as a black hoe, unless a trick spots her live and direct on the hoe stroll in action, he may be a bit hesitant with his approach 'cause he won't be sure if she's a gangsta bitch or a drug dealer's girlfriend. Therefore, a black hoe's catching game may not always be as simple as a white hoe's—but that doesn't make them less desirable.

There are plenty of beautiful black women whom the media allows the world to see. You got your supermodels, your TV stars, and your movie stars. The singers and the women who are dancers or extras in music videos.

Nowadays, they are seen about as often as white women who are attractive. And when a trick sees them in his search to pick up an attractive prostitute on the hoe stroll, they are just as much willing to deal with one of them as he would be with a white woman. That's if he hasn't had a disappointing encounter with a black hoe during a previous encounter.

Another thing that a trick looks for in a prostitute is an exotic feature. An Oriental woman with a big ass or thick with a nice shape is about the most exotic that it's going to get. A trick, or most men for that matter, would be overwhelmed to deal with that once-in-a lifetime experience, since a woman like that comes around as often as a woman giving birth to quintuplets. Just about any hoe that isn't black, but has an ass like a black woman is definitely going to receive a lot of benefits in her hoeing.

A lot of black hoes wear their hair blonde, and put contact lenses in their eyes to make them appear another color besides brown. For some reason, black women who are light skinned in the category of "yellow" or "red," have similar benefits as those of a white woman as far as breaking luck, and being easily approached by tricks. White women with a slim frame and big breasts are all right, but it's beginning to become as common as a black woman with a big ass. Big full lips on a white woman are becoming noticed as an exotic feature.

But for the most part, all pussy will sell. All a woman needs to sell pussy are two legs, a slit, a mouth to please and negotiate with! If a woman is attractive, a trick won't care if she's a substance abuser or not. They won't care what ethnicity she is. And he won't care what age she is. There are fifteen-year-old men who may get their dick sucked by a forty-five-year-old hooker. As long as he likes what he sees. There are prostitutes who come as young as twelve years old. Sure their makeup and high-heeled shoes will make them appear four or five years older than what they really are, but a trick doesn't have enough time to elaborate on what a woman's age is when he encounters her on the grounds of buying pussy. In addition, prostitutes don't have discrimination in their conduct. As far as how a guy looks is out the window.

Another thing limited in their conduct is passion. Veteran hoes, or at least ones with common sense will calculate just how far with a trick they'll go as far as intimacy. Anything that will lead up to a client having a misconception, such as tongue kissing, spending the night at his house without charging by the clock. Spending leisure time and going places and doing things that are more on a personal basis, instead of business, are the things that a hoe will try to avoid, 'cause they know what and where it will leave the client to misconceive.

The Reality

In the 1800s, there was an unidentified serial killer who was given the label "Jack the Ripper." The stomping grounds for his murders were in London, and his subjects were prostitutes. He would slash their throats and leave their corpse wherever they fall. More recently in our era, we had the I-40 killer, also known as Steven Pennel. He would drive around in a van that had a "rape kit" complete with restraints, whips, chains, and a branding iron. He would seek out prostitutes, torture them inside the van, then leave them lying on the side of the road. He admitted that his procedure was the appropriate one to do prostitutes "like the garbage they are."

It makes a person wonder, "Why would someone do this to another human being?" Well, there are two things people fear most in life—death and divorce. Death is something that no one has control over, and for the most part, accepts it as fate. As far as divorce or going separate ways with a spouse or loved one, it has much more of an emotional effect on the man than it does the woman.

Unless the man is well off financially, or of high status, his capabilities of coming across women who want to develop a solidified relationship with him will not be an opportunity that knocks at his door every five minutes. So now he has worries about being single and lonely, and not being able to find someone that he's compatible with.

As far as the woman, her ex-spouse will be well aware of her capabilities as a woman, as far as replacing him being no problem. Unless he has totally lost all feelings for her and was glad to see her go, his mind will go over disturbing fantasies of her involvement with another man. In the meantime, with his confidence being shaky as far as fully replacing her companionship-wise. Not until that moment comes, he will not get over her departure. Situations like this cause certain men to have a negative outlook on women. In another situation, there are men who have never experienced a relationship that they felt happy in. They have always envied other men who have a steady relationship with beautiful women, or a guy who has genuinely good luck with women without tricking. Although the overall picture may have a little bit to do with a feeling of jealously, the guy will more so blame women as a whole. He may feel that women are holding him accountable for a disadvantage of his, so therefore, "Fuck them all"!

The concept of prostitution becomes disturbing to him. Here he is having emotional dysfunctions with himself that he feels women placed on him by making his luck not appear to be so good, by giving authentic or falsified morals as to why they can't meet his expectations as a woman. Then you got prostitutes who have a different meaning of *moralistic*, and sex being superficial to them—nothing more than an avenue of business, an open game to any man who meets their financial criteria. This is hard for a man of one's nature to accept, and that is how they become disturbed.

It's momentarily accepted while the woman's prostitution is in his favor—since he's getting his dick sucked with a coke and a smile. But as soon as that episode is over, reality kicks him in the ass and reminds him that he isn't shit to the hooker. The same way she finessed him and sexed him up is the same way she's "done" many other men, and the same way she'll "do" many other men!

So here is this man who's dealing with insecurities. Face to face with a woman who sells sex for a living. A beautiful woman, more than likely. The kind he would rob a bank for, just to take her home and keep her for himself. But he knows it will never happen. He knows that her charm was all an act. Something that comes with her naturally in her line of work. So where does this leave this fella? To look at her like a piece of shit. An object instead of a person. His perception of her is to balance his insecurities. But that's not how he'll feel when he follows through with his cruel act toward the poor girl.

This is the way that most of these men evolve into a person who sees prostitutes as less than humans. It doesn't always start out on a tricking basis. It could be several different reasons from all types of men who was led to having dysfunctional feelings toward women, and the concept of prostitution didn't make it any better. What it did instead was give a sucker someone to take his problems out on that he feels is applicable—women!

That's why it is very necessary for a woman to develop a keen sense of reading a person for any symptoms of having this kind of potential. This is the worst kind of person that a prostitute can possibly encounter. In addition to that, a woman without strong male guidance can also use situations that she's come close to encountering on the basis of the aforementioned, and allow that to contribute to her reason for not liking men.

Women who survive through these types of encounters with these types of dudes tell stories of how they had to jump out of his vehicle naked and run down the street in that condition for help. How they may have had to jump out of the vehicle while it was in motion and got hurt, in fear of their life. Diving out of the way from a trick that is trying to run them over. Getting beat up and abused during sex, then not receiving any money at all, but rather being happy just to be alive. And several other life-threatening circumstances that these girls go through.

Most women that are sexually promiscuous would rather not have a man. It modifies their liberation, and gives them someone to explain themselves to. A woman, who is promiscuous is just like a man who is promiscuous. It comes with human nature. A lot of people feel that it is best to remain single, so that way, their sexual conduct won't affect anyone emotionally.

This is another reason why a lot of women who are prostitutes accept and appreciate pimps. A pimp is the total opposite of what a woman would expect to find in a man. He literally encourages them to have sex with other men. He contributes to their inner desire to want to remain sexually liberated. Then to top it off, a career is being carried out.

There's two different kinds of prostitutes overall. There are the "independent" ones. Then there's the "codependent" ones! And the difference between the two of them is that the codependent ones require guidance of some sort, while the independent ones function more on a solo basis. There's advantages and disadvantages with each one. I'm going to go over the matter of the independent ones first. Prostitutes who start off then remain independent were usually introduced to the art of prostitution without someone strongly encouraging them. Some had become successful right away without having a man involved to set an agenda for them. And the concept of prostitution was simply their choice.

They may have, in their beginning, come across a gentleman who gave them a financial offer in exchange for her leisure time, in an amount that she may not have ever had, or even seen, in her life. Without thinking twice about it, she jumped on the opportunity. Well, the business acquaintance between the two of them became a routine. And the metamorphosis of a prostitute began—without a pimp being involved.

The gentleman that she's dealing with may tell his friends, whose financial status is similar to his, and she'll have a larger clientele. She'll be more open with herself to take interest in other guys in regards to prostitution. If this was a woman who already obtained self-management skills, then she will see no use in giving her money to a man, or anyone for that matter, to manage for her. Once a woman has had a successful long-term experience on an independent basis when confronted by a pimp, she may understand the logic of his invitation, but will not feel that it applies to her. She is well aware of the

"codependent" kind of woman and believes in her heart that she is the total opposite.

An independent prostitute may, or may not, have a man. For the ones that do, the relationship between her and the guy will not be on some "boyfriend/girlfriend" shit.

'Cause she doesn't have enough time to set aside from her career to spend with him. Or would it be healthy for her to be in someone's presence too much, 'cause that's usually how feelings develop. The kind of man who would be able to serve her purpose, as far as companionship to whatever extent would be someone who isn't a trick, but isn't a pimp neither. The fella would be someone who she is "actually" attracted to, and doesn't elaborate or involve emotion in what she does. They're there to get each other off, then resume to normal program.

Self-dependendency and reliability in an independent prostitute also attracts other women to her in a manner of wanting to be introduced to a safe form of prostitution. This won't necessarily make the independent hoe think that she has pimping capabilities. However, by women coming to her in need of guidance to one extent or the other, her esteem will be very high.

But most of all, allow me not to leave this out—an independent prostitute can still be broken down into submitting to a pimp. Through pimpin', all things are possible when it comes to a prostitute! One of the good characteristics that is carried out by an independent hoe is they are a bit more reliable in certain situations. Especially with a man that they may be involved with to a certain extent. For example, let's say this kind of hoe has a male acquaintance that goes to jail. Her expectations to hold him down while he's in there will be a lot greater than a codependent hoe, who can easily be influenced by self-entertaining thoughts, or encouraged by others (especially men) to leave him hanging since he's not there to provide her with the guidance that she needs.

All independent hoes are not successful, and their categories vary. There are a lot of complex hoes that have never had a pimp, and they take the good along with the bad in their everyday experiences without the guidance of a man to help her balance out her misfortunes. This is the type of hoe who already feels sorry for herself for being a hoe, and she feels that having a pimp will only add insult to injury. Not to say that she dislikes men, but by not having one is an easy way for her to balance out her insecurities of prostituting.

She'll feel like she's better than a hoe that is with a pimp. Another form of an independent hoe is the tempered ones. This is the kind of hoe who has had a pimp before, but for whatever reason, that is no longer the case. Once the departure between her and her pimp occurs, she'll tell herself that "there is no other man who she will ever submit to, or do for, as her previous one."

Once they're in that frame of mind, they believe that they can just take what they learned while they were with their pimp, and survive off that. It will only be a matter of time before she misses having someone to submit to. Someone to call "daddy" and really mean it. Someone to refer to her as "bitch," who she feels it's his position, instead of that ol' "I love you, baby," and "good morning, sweetheart" bullshit that she hears from tricks day in and day out.

Once reality sets in on her that her independent effort, along with her half-ass definition of *loyalty* toward her former pimp, as far as not ever having another one, is only causing her to have cloudy days in the summertime, she'll eventually appreciate the first peek of sunshine that breaks through the clouds, and stay outside long enough to see the sky clear up. She will once again belong to a pimp, because she was a codependent hoe from the jump, and she tried to play something that wasn't her position.

Now, the codependent hoe. This is the one who keeps the game of pimps and prostitutes alive. She will not be able to successfully function without the guidance of a man. Unlike the independent hoe, she has, for the most part, had a man in her life in one degree or the other. She really hasn't been one to handle responsibilities like paying rent and similar things.

She's use to letting the man she's with take care of those types of things. All she does is serve his purpose by being his woman. In the case with one who belongs to a pimp, her purpose is to accumulate money in the field she's being guided in—which is prostitution—and let him take care of everything else.

The hoes who honestly know amongst themselves that they won't be able to function independently are the ones who accept and respect the concept of having a pimp. They have had plenty of experiences with downfalls and failures while trying to make it on their own. And in many situations, their initial encounter with a pimp happens to be at a time where they were going through hardship. Even though they were unstable residence-wise. Fresh out of jail. Living in some type of shelter, or group home. Being a runaway in traffic. Or a whole lot of other situations that caused her to accept an invitation of guidance.

A lot of codependent hoes have a self-esteem that is equivalent to an elevator in a tall building—it's "up and down" mileage meter is high. When they have a man—either a pimp or a slickster—that lets her do what she wants, her esteem is on the top floor. Being approached by a pimp, aside from the man she's already with, is like a joke to her. One of those "it'll never happen in a million fuckin' years" kind of mind frames.

Then as soon as something goes wrong inside her household that leads up to her walking down the street with a dirty bra strap, and her life's possessions squeezed into one bag that she's carrying, and she's approached by a pimp, her "I will never . . ." becomes exceptional. She'll accept his invitation if she's feeling him to some extent, then take it from there. This doesn't make this caliber of a hoe a bad person. She's only doing what her hand calls for—being under someone.

In the beginning of a lot of codependent hoes acquaintance with their pimps, the possibility of being "used" sometimes crosses their minds. Once they are broken all the way into accepting the concept that they are a part of a money-generating program, thoughts such as the aforementioned will exit their mind. They will soon recognize the luxuries, leisures, and conveniences that her work as a prostitute brings—unlike before. And in addition to that, she will take pride in her pimp and his money-managing skills.

Once a codependent hoe feels like her hoeing skills are bigger than life, then a conflict occurs between her and the man she works for, her mind may tend to entertain the thought of functioning successfully on an independent basis if she decides to run off. Most of the time, when effort is put forth to actually do so, it doesn't last. She becomes equivalent to a stray dog that needs to find its way back home. The phrase "out of sight, out of mind" plays largely in that kind of hoe.

They take an infatuated liking toward the one(s) who can support them on immediate grounds. All the has-been persons, places, and things become irrelevant, unless the boomerang effect takes place—by her bumping heads with a previous source of guidance at a time when she's in need.

There is an old pimp phrase that goes, "A chicken ain't nothing but a bird, and a hoe won't keep her word"! Codependent hoes more so brought the logic of that phrase to life. Within their own guidelines of circumstances, a hoe will lay with any man; therefore, she'll be with any man. In life, everyone has to answer to someone whether a building manager, a landlord, the IRS, the police, a mother during one's stage of childhood, or a nigga with a gun pointed to your head. And 99 percent of people need some type of assistance because the world doesn't revolve on a one-man-show basis. But the thing with a codependent woman, she literally needs someone to take her by the hand and guide her through her steps. It's similar to the concept of a young child and the parent.

Unlike a pimp, a prostitute cannot hoe all her life. There is no age bracket with pimping, since it is a trade that requires intelligence and management skills, not necessarily beauty. Prostitution requires being attractive, which, in most cases, comes with youth, along with a personality to help the "catching" part of the game. As a hoe ages, her beauty may deteriorate, to where all she has left as an advantage is her personality. (Which doesn't get old.)

Women who believe that they can hoe until the wheels fall off usually lead themselves to a disappointment. True indeed that they have their pussy to fall back on whenever necessary. But who's going to want to pay for a bitch that's sixty years old? Sure, all pussy sells, but I doubt seriously if a woman up there in years will be able to accumulate enough money to maintain what we call a "living."

Old crackhead bitches and junkie bitches that are seen on an often basis in an inner-city neighborhood had at sometime in their younger years indulged in a career of prostitution; to whatever extent, it varies. Some had pimps. Some did the independent thing, and others did a little bit of everything. Not to say that every older drug addict woman has once lived a life of prostitution, but there are very many who had.

Most people who indulge in a lifestyle that brings fast money and free of taxes should allow themselves to be aware that it is rare for it to be a life-term success.

The ones who develop skills in an area where their money isn't considered unlawfully earned are the ones who have a shot at longevity. For the women who do believe that there pussy has a lifetime guarantee for prostituting, it's not necessarily true. With the dysfunctional emotions that can be activated in a prostitute at any given moment, their results may differ from any man who doesn't have his head on right.

Men will not resort to a lot of things that are driven by stress, because their pride won't allow them to. For example, a hoe has a fucked-up day. She's out and about, dwelling in the inner city where there are drug dealers, users, gangbangers, and all that good shit which makes up that environment. She gets around a crowd of smokers who's letting her cry her heart out and listening to her, because she has a purse full of money. Then the next thing you know, she's talking about, "Fuck it! Let me take a hit of that shit."

At that moment, she will be considered to have signed a life-term contract to be a drug addict by means of sticking a needle in her arm, or sucking on a glass dick. What makes her not hesitate to follow through with her decision is her course of short thinking and a lack of self-discipline.

This example is mostly found in a codependent kind of hoe in particular. Just like a child who runs away from home, a codependent hoe was emotionally driven to see if she can hang on an independent basis, and what happens? The world bites her in the ass! She becomes a guppy in a lake full of piranha, and gets her ass gobbled up!

She doesn't mind taking a hit of some crack, or slamming some dope in her arms for the first time.

Besides, any complexities about it, is well balanced out beforehand. She sucks off at least ten guys a day, and has more dicks running through her ass than toilet paper. So what difference is it going to make to her mentally if she enters the world of crackheads and junkies?

Her hoeing will never be the same, and neither will a whole lot of other things about her. But as far as she's concerned, it's mind over matter. If she doesn't mind, it doesn't matter. That's the fate of the majority of dysfunctional hoes. As far as the chances of them experiencing prison, the small percentage of the ones who will, will more than likely be multiple-time drug offenders.

Pimps who become drug addicts evolve in a totally different manner than a hoe. First of all, being one who masters the art of managing women's emotions for them, a pimp won't be one to pick up a crackpipe or needle due to being in a stressed-out frame of mind. Their drug usage usually starts off as being an activity. Something they see along the lines of leisure. There are not very many complexities involved with sniffing cocaine. Especially if he has the income that he believes will back him up.

Well, they say that "one drug leads to another," and in many situations, that's the reason for promotion in a nonbeneficial manner. However, unlike the prostitute, the odds of a pimp experiencing prison are greater than one becoming a drug addict. Statistics-wise, there are more junkie/junkie hoes, than there are junkie/junkie pimps. And there are more incarcerated, or has been incarcerated pimps, than there are incarcerated, or has been incarcerated hoes!

A codependent prostitute without guidance is like a blank canvas that takes a trip through a paint store. It's vulnerable to every and any can of paint that it comes across. By the time the canvas leaves the store, it will look as if someone painted skittles on it. Some hoes simply just give up. Their desires in life are limited. The drug addicted ones live on a "get high, get by" basis.

When a pimp lays out a format in front of them that they know would be perfect for them, the hoe would rather die than to accept the opportunity. It has nothing to do with the pimp personally. It has to do with themselves, and the fact of how they gave up.

This testimony is not intended to discriminate to any extent. But rather to voice the raw reality of what some go through, what some been through, and what some have seen. The same fate does not await every prostitute on whatever status on particular grounds. Or should the intelligence of a prostitute be underestimated due to their sexual conduct. His or her intelligence varies just like anyone else's. Only difference is, for prostitutes who are unguided, or misguided, their intelligence is irrelevant to their conduct, unless they have someone to activate it for them.

Hoeing is a mood. Depending on what frame of mind a woman is in will determine on her conduct while she's out working. If she's under a pimp, and the matter is on shaky grounds in the house, once she's out of his sight, she will be less hesitant to blow up. If she's in a good mood, with her esteem-boosted sky high while she's out the door and on her way to work, her performance will more than likely bring beneficial results.

But if the mood happens to be the other way around, while out there working, and she decides not to run off, they might at the least pull an act of absence, doing things like not answering the cell phone, hiding out somewhere that she knows her pimp won't discover her, then appearing after a long period of time has gone by once she's gained the nerve plus the courage to face up to her misconduct.

One of the most common ways that a person describes a prostitute when one comes to mind is *immoral*. However, this interpretation is not necessarily true. While moralizing someone upon one's own judgment, they are not aware that "morals" deal with virtues and ethics. *Immoral* is not an adequate classification for a woman who is sexually promiscuous. A sexually promiscuous woman can have many ethics.

For example: Here's a woman who has experience in pornography. She has a foot in the door in the world of adult entertainment. From time to time, she goes to photo sessions. She does some porno shots with a dick in her mouth, with male semen spread across her face. At the same time, she has a dick in her pussy and another one up her asshole. But when that session is over, she goes home with the money she made and meets the expectations of a responsible adult. How the money was made is irrelevant to her conduct of responsibilities.

Another example: Here's a woman with a pimp. Her conduct as far as sex is definitely not chaste, or celibate. However, her every move in her conduct as a prostitute is to honestly succeed the expectations that she long ago agreed upon with her pimp. She is loyal to him, as well as honorable, and her conduct for those reasons alone classifies her as having virtues.

When someone thinks of a woman who is opened with her sexuality, and they try to think of her as being immoral, it's only because they're "aware" of her sexual conduct. They refuse to give her the benefit of the doubt that aside from her sexual conduct, she may be a great person at heart. But they'll make what they believe to be an accurate judgment about the woman who works at the supermarket, 'cause every time they see her behind the cash register, she's exercising good manners and politeness to all the customers—including him!

If ever she were to come to mind, she is sure to have a halo above her head. But the ones who's making this judgment is not thinking about the possibility of her sexual conduct. Why? Because more than likely, it revolves around which would be considered her "personal life."

But regardless if it's her personal life or not, for all he knows, guys may have had more turns with her than a doorknob to a public restroom. Let's say that in addition to that, she steals money out of the cash register, because her boss is some old dumbfuck who'll probably never catch on. So there you have it. A woman who has more moralistic strikes against her than a prostitute—she's sexually promiscuous, she's unethical to her nine-to-five, and her virtues fall short by being a petty thief. Mr. Unaware Square is not aware of all that; she's an all right girl in his eyes compared to the "immoral" prostitute.

But that just goes back to what I said earlier about people being disturbed with the concept of prostitution. What people fail to realize is that prostitution, to whatever extent, enables a woman to become open with her sexuality, unlike before where she may have had complexities or insecurities.

As I also previously mentioned in this book, when it comes to acceptance, most people will open themselves up to a lot of things that they were once unsure of. If a woman once viewed the general concept of prostitution as degrading, she can easily have her mind shifted in the direction of accepting it if she were to ever encounter other women who are active prostitutes in high esteem of what they do.

Especially if the encounter includes a pimp, which at all times will possess a demeanor of high spirits. For a woman to be surrounded by all this at once, with it totally transgressing against any sexual complexities she may have ever had, she will definitely surrender her will to taking interest in a program that she would have never imagined existed.

Mommy, daddy, little sister, big brother, Mr. Nice Guy who works at the local fast-food restaurant, the college teacher, the previous boyfriend, the current boyfriend, the square female friends, and everyone else who would more than likely not take the matter of her becoming a little whore lightly, would be pushed all the way out of the picture and her mind once she's came across an invitation to be a part of a program that has answers, alternatives, and solutions to any and all her insecurities.

On a whole other note, true indeed that if a hoe will lay with any man, she'll be with any man. But the science to that is this here. A hoe will give anybody some pussy, but as far as submitting to someone to the fullest extent, the concept of having a pimp to pay for his guidance is as accurate as she's going to find.

Sure there are plenty of guys who will treat her like a queen. But if sex and companionship is the best way to repay them (being as superficial as it already is) it will soon get played out. By a man's intention to expand no further than to basically surrender all his dignity to a hoe, she will eventually feel deep in her spirit that something isn't right about that, and end up losing respect for the guy. The next thing you'll know, she'll be in desire of a boss, and want that sucker to get lost.

Many hoes, not only the complex ones, they accept the task of being a prostitute like a crack smoker, by giving themselves false hope not to die in their ways! Hardcore drug addicts and hookers alike tell themselves during their evolving stages that they're just doing what they do for a little while. Considering themselves as being on vacation. Trying to keep themselves convinced that they have the power to shut it down any time they want to, and a whole lot of other insecurity balancing thoughts that they entertain.

Well, that "turn on, turn off" vacation that they assured themselves at the beginning of their escapade ends up being something that is only turned off by force. Like getting arrested, while incarcerated—ain't shit happening. Nevertheless, most drug addicts and prostitutes alike feel that their circumstances as one are "exceptional."

Believe it or not, prostitution is becoming a fad. Just like the media has its ways with projecting its image of a so-called pimp to the public eye, it does the same for prostitutes. Young minds have a tendency to admire something that they're fond of in the entertainment industry. They play out thoughts in their mind of something pertaining to their own life coinciding with celebrities.

For example, there are thousands of young black men throughout the country who feel that they have a little 2 PAC in them. There may be a movie with a person's favorite actor or actress in it; and then in addition to that, the story the movie was based on happens to have something in common with the person who watched it. All of a sudden, here comes the fantasies being played out of how that person will think that the actor/actress and oneself have something in common.

The modern-day media makes prostitution and similar things that revolve around it look more influential then ever. Lets take the movie *Pretty Woman* for example, which starred Julia Roberts. She is a top-of-the-line actress, so it is only obvious that she has an influence on people, particularly white girls. A young lady may see that movie and think that prostitution is the thing to do, since Julia Roberts played the role as one. While all along missing the point that it was only a character played out by a professional actress.

Then you got the rapper Lil Kim, who openly raps about promiscuity and her acceptance of it. That, along with her style of dress code, has an influence on young black women and young ladies of other ethnicities who listen to rap music. They see Lil Kim making millions off of the image she portrays through her lyrics and demeanor, and play out a fantasy in their mind that tells them that "if Lil Kim is successful and accepted by her overall image, then everything she's representing is all right."

They even go further into thinking that they can possibly become as successful as she is if they live through the things that they believe Lil Kim lived through. Things that are also seen through the media have an effect on young women's conduct and esteem as well.

Back to the days of the *I Love Lucy Show*, television has evolved into a subliminal consent of semi x-rated contents. On the show, Lucy and Ricky were never seen lying together in the same bed. In their bedroom, their beds were always separated. Then a couple of decades later, a TV show comes on the air known as *The Dukes of Hazard*, in which there's a female character by the name of Daisy Dukes.

She was the first one to break the barrier of cut-off jeans being worn upper thigh high, and made the style famous to the extent of it being named after her character. Viewers who admired her would watch the show in hopes of getting a glimpse of the bottom of her ass cheeks hanging out of the shorts.

Then a couple of decades after that, the TV show *Bay Watch* came about, with Pamela Anderson running around with some big ass titties flying everywhere. Then everything after that, as far as TV shows, generally known magazines and music videos of all types have become semi x-rated at the least, and semi-pornography at the most. A person doesn't necessarily have to watch a porno flic, or flip through a porno magazine to be encouraged by sex. The point I'm making is this: as I mentioned several times already, "acceptance."

Many things that the media projects falls on the eyes and mind of a person (particularly women) that are vulnerable, due to being young at age, having an unbalanced esteem, or simply fascinated by those whom they allow to be a role model for them. Set aside from the media setting the impression upon those who are open game to it, many women already had it (prostitution) in them. All they needed for their insecurity to be balanced out was something, someone, or some reason for it to be brought up out of them.

Another thing that differs hoes by their ethnicities are their sexual conduct with their pimps. Although there are characteristics that can be specifically found in one race of women, there are exceptional circumstances to where a certain characteristic may be found in a woman outside of the race specified.

A lot of hoes have their own way of testing their man through sex. Many white hoes like to do the "Kiss of Test" with their man. This is when they suck on their man's dick, then raise up with intentions to kiss him on the mouth. If the man allows her to follow all the way through with her intentions, by contributing to the kiss, she will go along with it while she is lost in the mind state of the so-called "lovemaking." But after that episode is over, she will collect her thoughts of what her motive was in the first place, and hold that strike against her man as a weakness.

Besides, no matter how long a hoe is with her pimp, she will always think deep down in the back of her mind that "all men are the same." And by a pimp giving in to that test by failing it, he will be unknowingly catering to that thought. A white hoe, being someone who is already opened to a lot of different sex acts, occasionally experience tricks who want her to stick her finger up their ass while she sucks them off. Although this is usually kept to herself, it still and all has a personal effect on her judgment of how far a man will go with his sexual indulgence. So she's thinking, if one out of every ten tricks wants a finger stuck up his ass, why not test her man with something small to start out with, such as the "Kiss of Test"?

Now as far as the black hoe and the conduct with her man, her testing is through deficiency. They enjoy playing on their man's desire to have sex at his will. They may say some shit about how they don't want to suck his dick upon his request, 'cause that's what she does with tricks all day long. Whatever it is in sexual regards between her and her man, she will find a transgression to it. If she sees her pimp isn't the type who cares much for having sex with her, she'll even use that to play on.

"Daddy, can we please have sex before I go to work?" And then go further into coming up with a reason why she feels it's necessary. As soon as her pimp hits her with the "purse first, ass last" response of why it isn't going to happen, she'll use that to get an attitude. But in a case where her pimp decides to honor her recommendation and have sex with her, she will throw an attitude in the air that she's in a position to do things at her will when her pimp tells her to hit the door.

All pimps and hoes do not go through this during their acquaintances. But there are plenty who have. Another thing about many hoes of all kinds, they are trapped in a mind frame which causes their personality to reflect as being five to ten years younger than their actual age. This is caused by the lack of responsibilities that they didn't have to face when they chose to allow sexual dependency as a way of getting by.

Many hoes have a childlike instinct. Things like being desired, drawing attention, being playful, and seeking acceptance fascinate them. Of course, these characteristics are carried out in an environment that they feel comfortable in. Through time, a lot of their childlike characteristics began to fade away as they experience certain incidents in life, in which their response had to consist of seriousness.

For those who become drug addicts or those who experience long-term imprisonment, either consecutively or off and on, their childlike characteristics quickly vanish from their conduct. They will by then find it necessary to let go to avoid being perceived as vulnerable and becoming a victim. Once this phase of a hoe's life has occurred, things that were once viewed by them as pleasant or fascinating will no longer exist.

Many events that they'll face in life will leave them in the mind frame of being miserable. They will also become harder to subdue. A lot of people become disturbed with the concept of younger women being with a gentleman who is older than them. In most cases, younger men who witness a pimp who is in his late twenties on up, with girls who are obviously younger than him are the ones who allow themselves to feel disturbed. Reason being, they may feel as if their capabilities of getting younger women who are in their age bracket should be more advanced than a guy who is older. What they fail to realize is the young women who are with a pimp that is older than them are prostitutes. They are not looking for a young man to be with in an adolescent-like relationship, which consist of things like going to the movies, tongue kissing, holding hands in public, free fucking day and night, trying to make a baby, lying side by side in the bed facing each other and blowing smoke up one another's ass of how "It'll last forever," while there's some R&B music playing in the background.

Most of those young ladies had already been there and done that! Once they stepped into the world of prostitution, the chances of them returning to that type of lifestyle is very rare. Like Jay-Z said in his tune "Song Cry," "once a good girl's gone bad, she's gone forever." It takes a different kind of man to attract these women to him as a dependable figure.

In other situations, there are pimps who themselves are young, and at times may have a hoe or two who is older than him. But in a situation like this, age is not important. Young pimps are usually equipped with the same knowledge and physiological intelligence of one who is older than him. Therefore, that leaves a hoe to still look at him as an older type of figure, and there will be no difference in the conduct of their program.

As a matter of fact, a lot of hoes who have a pimp who is younger than them feel somewhat honored by being desired by a younger man. Just like older hoes feel honored to have clients who are younger men. In addition to a woman being up under a pimp who is older than her, looks is not what necessarily attracts her to him. The way men see women as a beautiful being, which is the cause of her companionship having a price tag on it, is not equivalent to the perception that women have on men. If a woman finds a man that she's with as visually attractive, then that is considered a bonus for her. What attracts women to men (hoes to pimps in particularly) is their status, materialistic possessions, and personality. Also she can be supported by his acquaintance on immediate grounds.

The relationship between a woman and a man under such circumstances varies. It is not only for pimps and prostitutes. It can be with a sugar daddy and a hoe. It could be with a young woman who always took interest in older men, instead of one in her age group, 'cause she enjoys having someone to look to as a father figure along with being her man. Or it could simply be a hoe that is on a date with a trick that is of any age much older than her own.

So when a person on a regular basis witnesses a young lady with an older man, who may be perceived as a mismatch by their appearance, aside from the age difference, sometimes it is what it seems, and sometimes it isn't. But either way, it's no accident.

Different hoes are equally turned off and turned on with different approaches from pimps. All approaches will not work on just any hoe. There are a lot of hoes who will feel either offended or agitated by the approach from pimps who talk fast with enthusiastic lines. Then there's those who love it, and just got to have it! Then there's women who are approached by pimps that may be a bit thrown off by somewhat of an intellectual approach. This will either cause the hoe to become confused and not want to take any interest. Or it can cause them to become curious, since "whatever the hell he's talking about" sounds right, although she isn't necessarily sure what it means.

Sometimes it's not necessarily what the pimp is saying that catches a hoe's curiosity, but rather the confidence that she notices in his person that causes her to take interest. Sometimes, during the beginning of an acquaintance between a prostitute and a pimp, the hoe feels somewhat in the state of shock. Something like a wild animal being domesticated. They momentarily dislike their pimp subconsciously 'cause they feel as if they've been robbed for their liberation. What they were used to doing at their own discretion is no longer the case.

They are now involved in a program with rules to abide by. Some hoes are not patient enough to stay down for the man they work for until they see what benefits they'll receive from having a pimp, as opposed to their previous occupation. In many cases, the ones who do put forth effort to stay down for their pimps will test his tolerance level to see how far they can go. One of the many ways that they go about their testing is by purposely allowing things to interfere with the conduct of their expectations.

During a slow moment of their shift, where they're having a hard time breaking luck, they make sure that their pimp becomes aware of this, and try to use that as a reason to see if he'll have the generosity to lift her up off the track at his consent. Another testing method they will use with the same intentions is the old "rape" gimmick—specifically by telling their pimp that one of the tricks during their shift had "forcibly" fucked them and didn't give them a dime in Chinese money.

Most of the time when a hoe is claiming that alleged accusation against a trick, they don't have a scratch on them, or any apparent sign for that matter to assist them with their "story." Once more, it was only a test in hopes of finding leniency in their pimp.

First of all, a hoe hollering "rape" is like a boxer crying about getting hit in the face. Second of all, if a hoe is talking about how slow it is and how she can't break luck, by her making a request to her pimp to be lifted off of the track is an obvious test. Nine times out of ten, if that same hoe was a heroin addict without a pimp and she was selling her ass to get her next fix so she won't have to deal with being dope sick, she would stay her ass out there like the world was coming to an end until she catches a date.

The thing is this, if a pimp allows a hoe of his to receive leniency upon her reason and will, she will go further into the test by trying to see how many of the same benefits she'll still receive from her pimp, even though her productive expectations were not up to par. As a result to this, the hoe will eventually lose respect for her pimp and leave him under the "guilt free" circumstances.

As far as she will be concerned, he has failed the test—of meeting the expectations that a hoe will always have embedded in their minds that "all men are the same," as far as giving in to her, or meeting her halfway on a rule that should be strictly enforced by the man and him alone.

The hoe will sense a sign of fear in her pimp, on the basis of her thinking that he gives in to her—whether he knows she's full of shit or not—cause he may not want to lose her as his working bitch. In many situations, the hoe would have had more respect for her pimp if he had enforced his authority at the times when she tried to manipulate her way into leniency. Not necessarily by being an all-out asshole, but more in a finessing style of assurance that his way of doing things is the only way and should not be objected. In other words, like they say, "Hoe up, or blow up," "Be about it, or be without it."

A pimp has better indications of when it's necessary for certain procedures to be taken out there on the hoe stroll than a hoe does. In many situations, women become paranoid. Once a pimp gives a hoe a thorough rundown of the awareness he has of all the possible excuses that she can ever come up with in an effort to receive leniency on a testing basis, she'll respect his intelligence, or she'll get the hell away from him 'cause she'll know that he isn't one to be easily fooled with bullshit.

For the ones who respect him for his intelligence and stay down for him, they will see him as an exception—as opposed to many other men they've encountered in life—and feel comfortable going over matters of truth with him, instead of fabricating a story. Some may be selectively honest. And other forms of honesty may be modified. But the pimp would be receiving more honesty out of that hoe than she felt any other man has ever been entitled to. Reason being, a hoe respecting her man for his intelligence is giving a very strong sense of respect. If a hoe were to lie about something, or keep something to herself that she knows her pimp would be better off knowing about, and he were to believe her dishonesty, it would seriously play on her conscience, and she would not feel right looking this man in the eyes, of whom she respects for his intelligence.

In addition to that, one of the many things that a hoe appreciates is having someone to be honest with. Someone she can be herself around and be accepted for it by all means.

While this bitch may see everyone else in the world as not being entitled to her honesty, her pimp may be the only exception.

Another thing about hoes and their selective honesty: any woman who has ever once familiarized herself with prostitution to whatever extent can be approached by a pimp who has the intention to recruit her, and admit that she indulged in prostitution before in her life. Then, on the other hand, she can be in a relationship with a man who is square to the pimping and prostitution game for a significant amount of time and never share the information with him of her once being a prostitute throughout their entire relationship.

Many hoes feel as if submitting to a pimp is tampering with their personal life. Interfering with the things that they would rather be doing if most of their time wasn't being put into their life of prostitution. In most situations, they'll feel that way until they begin to recognize the benefits of their newfound career. Once they feel that the activity they indulge in, in their line of duty outweight their former activities, they'll be more at ease with the overall concept.

Sometimes, depending on the hoe, this process may take hours, days, and sometimes weeks for a hoe to make this determination. If the woman feels that her newfound program is suitable for her, she will stay, and her pimp will consider himself having her in "checkmate." If for whatever reason she doesn't, she will blow up.

For some unknown reason, in which science may not ever be able to explain, prostitutes and/or drug-addicted women tend to believe that they love the man responsible for turning them out to be what they are.

Even if it was done in a cruel an unfair manner, they do not hold him accountable, and accept it as if that's what their hand was called for.

Let me not forget to mention that sexually transmitted diseases play a large role in the possibility of being contracted during her line of duty. Some hoes are carefree and believe that there is no harm in giving a guy a blow job without a condom being placed on his penis. For the ones who think like that, the only suggestion I would make would be to talk to another hoe who is HIV positive who never had general intercourse with a client without protection, but thought it was cool to be a "semen demon" and gave blow jobs to bare-back penises.

There are even tricks out there who caught STD from unknown prostitutes and their goal is to give it back to as many of them as possible. Sometimes when a hoe unknowingly encounters this kind of trick, and she's the kind who practices all of the safe sex precautions, and makes it clear to her client that she "will not" indulge in any type of sex with him without the use of a condom, he'll see to it that his goal is still accomplished, either through trickery or by force.

And vice versa. There are even hoes out there who contracted STD from unknown tricks, and their mission is to return the favor to any and all of them that she comes in contact with. This type of woman is very crafty with condoms in the way that she manipulates her clients to believe that they're "protected," when they really aren't.

However, this does not make all hoes and clients bad people. Just like one bad pimp doesn't spoil the whole game due to a malfunction in his individuality.

Tricks and clients are the third party in the game of pimping and prostitution. Without them, or any man who's willing to pay for a woman for that matter, the game as it is would not exist. They are as important to the game, as Big Mac and french fry consumers are to McDonald's. As crack smokers are to crack dealers. And as an audience is to concert.

It would take an immature mind, especially if one is supposed to be a pimp, to look down on a man for buying pussy. The majority of the people who would be critical of this matter for the purpose of entertainment and recreation would more than likely be the ones who pay for pussy themselves, but would refuse to see it that way. They would say that what they do is considered "treating," but the sophisticated man who pays top dollar for bona fide hookers is "tricking."

There isn't any difference. If there's a nigga in the inner city who smokes crack, and has a nice enough portion to "party" with throughout the night. Then he decides to have to have a young cute bitch in his company that gets high also, to join him at his expense. All along while he's dicking this hoe down, he's tricking. But he won't see it like that. Maybe because he's not paying her with actual cash. But regardless of what he's giving her, she's still being paid with something she accepts in exchange for her sexual services. And if it were for any other reason besides that, she would not be there.

Same goes for the drug dealers who trick off the crumbs in the corner of their sack of rocks with an attractive female addict. And even for the scenario in the lowest common denominator, where a man wines a woman in all usual aspects, at his expense, just for a chance to get some pussy—which isn't even guaranteed. He's tricking with a 50/50 chance motive, but like I've mentioned several times throughout this book, people pay for what they want! So when it comes to tricking, there is no major or minor. Felony or misdemeanor. Hot or cold. If a woman is not indulging in sex with a man solely because she likes him for him, and his penis is to her, what her vagina is to him, then the one doing the tricking is whoever that's paying.

The only time that tricking should be looked at as "degrading" to one's own self is when a person is really hurting himself or herself financially, materialistically, or spiritually to pay for some pussy. However, that rarely occurs not to say that it doesn't happen. Characteristics are more commonly found in drug addicts. For a man who has a hard time getting pussy, there is a traditional alternative—pornography, imagination, and masturbation; but for a drug addict, there is no alternative for getting high, but the high itself.

When society views the overall concept of the pimping and prostitution trade, they see it only one way: the pimp being on the top of the food chain as the bad guy, and the prostitute being his victim by being exploited by him. They view the tricks and clients as the prostitute's victims by making her unconditionally desired bait that takes advantage of the lust that many men are unable to control just because she's available—for a fee. What society fails to realize is that all the participants are involved by choice—not force! A man takes it upon his own will to pay a woman for her sexual willingness, to relieve his desire.

A prostitute gives her pimp the money to manage 'cause she appreciates him for not leaving her unprovided or misguided. He has a job that no other man would be able to handle if his life depended on it. Without pimps, or any applicable source of guidance for a prostitute, the appreciated ones would not be the same women the world knows them as.

Closing Commentary

Young people go to school to become educated. Once they've become adults, some of the things that they once learned becomes unimportant to them, mainly because there is no use for that particular knowledge in their field. However, it is still a piece of information that was downloaded in their brain.

If they took geometry and learned how to measure the circumference of a circle by multiplying pie (3.14) times the diameter, they'll get their answer. There is no other formula to use to get the correct measurement of a circle's circumference. Just like there is only one formula to the pimping-and-prostitution trade, no other formula will make it equal to the correct answer. However, pimping and prostitution is not taught in the American education system. It is because schools do not want to be responsible for little girls in the classroom raising their hand and saying, "I want to be a prostitute or porno star when I grow up."

They sure as hell got something to keep children from saying, "I want to be a dope fiend when I grow up." A young child in school wouldn't dare say that, for the simple fact that schools throughout the nation have drug-awareness programs, leaving a young and developing mind to think against it. But they don't have anything to teach them about pimps and prostitutes. The closest thing they have to that is "sex education," which is taught in high school. Is it 'cause they don't want it to appear as if they're corrupting a child's mind? Or is it 'cause the educators feel that by ignoring the fact, chances are the kids may not ever become aware of that. A child in elementary school will be taught what the use of a hypodermic needle's narcotic purpose is, but will have to learn somewhere down the line in some other regards from school what a pimp and prostitute is.

Schools give "drug awareness" to young kids to prevent them from becoming drug addicts. But do they give "prostitution awareness" classes to young ladies to prevent them from becoming one? Of course, they don't! Why not? Because indirectly and submentally, it's acceptable. Why is it that a person, male or female, has to be eighteen years of age to indulge in prostitution in its legal forms—such as pornography, or some sort of tax-paying service—but has to wait until they're twenty-one years of age to legally purchase alcohol? They'll take a willing female, and count down to the second she turns eighteen like they're bringing in a New Year, just to use rolls and rolls of film to take pictures of her with her ass spread wide open for the world to see—with or without something stuffed up in it. What would the argument be with the age-comparison matter in purchasing alcohol?

"The young 'consenting' adult female wasn't a virgin when she entered the porno industry." Well shit, the young consenting gentleman wasn't no sober fella up until he was old enough to buy a drink. Just like the young woman was already sexually active by the time she came around, a young teenaged fella had been sending someone else in the liquor store for him, who had an ID to purchase alcohol. What's the best logic to justify that? They don't want to legally consent people under the age of twenty-one consuming alcohol because it will interfere with the physical and health development of an immature body. Hell, if they think that entertaining sexual promiscuity is any healthier, then somebody's not thinking clearly.

But truth of the matter is, a woman was born with her vagina to do what she wants to do with it—and the shit is acceptable, like I already said. If worldwide statistics were to be done on the number of people who are consumers of dangerous, mind-altering substances—such as narcotics—and the number of people who are in sexual desire of woman, the drug matter would look like a marble standing next to the basketball-sized lust of men, and a few girls, who are in desire for the female specimen. Pussy and its value was around way before drugs, and will always outweigh them.

Prostitution being "illegal" is only a front that America puts up to cater to the disturbed citizens that drive to work every morning and have to see woman on the street with their dresses lifted halfway up ass cheeks, waving to men driving by on their way to start their day. Furthermore, the street level of prostitution is also considered "illegal" 'cause the police are aware that an unemployed pimp, or non-tax-paying drug dealer, or both, is living off of their earnings. But as soon as it's done in a fashion that a "Broke Nigger" isn't profiting off of it—such as pornography, call girls services, and tax paying whorehouses—it's all right, and America loves it!

As I had already mentioned about the circumference of a circle and the formula used to get it, which will always be remembered, the formula of the pimp game can be explained, but one will continue to refuse to accept it for what it is—either by choice or ignorance. The three things that the media has promoted throughout the years in an effort to make it appear to be acceptable to America is profanity, prostitution, and homosexuality. The pimp, on the other hand, is becoming more and more defaced through the media by the day. Once upon a time, television-broadcasting headquarters would edit out any profanity before the program was aired.

Then throughout the decades, the word *damn* became common, and not necessarily looked at as profanity. However, it is still prohibited in courtrooms, and not to be used by children, in front of teachers, and other adult figures. Same for the word *ass*, which has become almost as common as the word *hello*. Then came the word *bitch*. You can watch just about any TV show on UPN and hear that word flying out of actors' and actresses' mouths as if they're getting a one-hundred-dollar bonus for every time they say it.

It took the FCC long enough to catch on that such TV shows that contained profanity material were accessible to children simply by turning on the TV in the mid-nineties; the barrier was broken for publicized homosexuality on a very famous TV talk show when two lesbian women were tongue kissing. From that moment on, publicized homosexuality took off like a rocket. Everything—from gay conduct in the music industry, to watching TV talk shows with a whole lot of transvestites having fun like they're at a "gay parade." When young children see this on their TV set, it is not arguable that there's a chance and possibility of these children perceiving that kind of material to be acceptable.

But regardless of what negative influence America has on the vulnerable minds of the young children, it is still not being objected. A lot of the ways that prostitution is being directly and indirectly promoted has already been mentioned throughout the "Prostitute" section of this book. But when it comes to a pimp, it is not in any fashion, form, or figure glorified or glamorized by the media (with the exception of a few rap songs that were fictitiously created by people who never lived the life of a pimp).

Instead, it is degraded since the beginning of the millennium; there has been a major motion picture dropped every other year, which included a pimp character whose role was intended to demoralize the image. In 2001, there was *How High*. In 2003, there was *Friday after Next*. I had already covered those in the "Pimp" section of this book. But the one I didn't cover yet was 2005's *Deuce Bigalow: European Gigolo*.

In that movie, in which the actor Eddie Griffin costarred, he played the role as a pimp who had male gigolos in his stable, instead of women.

(In which the movie script referred to them as "prostitutes.") His character throughout the movie consisted of him being a complex and/or potential homosexual. At the end of the movie, after he was released out of jail and relieved but not being sexually assaulted while he was inside, he had changed his career from being a gigolo's pimp to a "gay man's" pimp—and his stable of drag queens were nearby.

Now as funny as it may be, if a person is looking for the humor of the matter, the overall picture is still being overlooked. Why is it that the media will use national television syndicates to promote real live homosexuality and make it appear to be acceptable, but go so far out of their way to demoralize the face of the pimp that they'll use imaginary scenarios? If a thirteen-year-old youngster sees that movie—and that's the only perception of a pimp that that young person has ever had—best believe that when that person becomes a little older and ends up in a conversation about a pimp, that person will only be able to recall what was in a movie like that.

In the early nineties, the movie *King of New York* had a scene where a pimp was assassinated while standing in a public phone booth, 'cause "he had thirteen-year-old girls out there selling their ass." So the point I'm making is this: the thing that triggers a screenwriter's motive to produce this type of material is the traditional dislike toward pimps. Screenwriters have been making a lot of money by creating updated versions of movies that were from an era or two ago. Movies like *Shaft* and *Carlito's Way*. But why haven't they made an update version of the movie *The Mack*? Because they do not want the public to view a pimp as someone who is entitled to respect.

Instead, they'll take movies like *Carlito's Way*, make an update version, using a hip hop icon like Sean "P. Diddy" Combs as a costar, and allow the story to end with all the drug dealers coming out smelling like roses, after they swam through a lakeful of shit. If Americans believe that a movie like that has more of a positive influence on a young mind, as opposed to the reality of what a pimp is, they're crazy!

But, of course, movies like that will continue to be publicized through the media for the simple fact that the screenwriters know more people will be able to relate to it. There are more young black men, as well as other minority groups, who have experienced selling drugs, than there are men who sent a woman to walk up and down the street and sell her ass for him.

A lot of people tend to entertain the thought of a pimp being a soft kind of guy. That thought comes to different people's minds, for different reasons. Set aside from the people who are innocent of their perception of what a pimp may be, due to their limited exposure being expanded no further than their television set, there are plenty of people who have come across pimps and acquainted themselves to one extent or the other, to where they feel like they "know" a pimp, and they'll still refuse to see someone who is equal to them "tough" wise.

A lot of niggas from the hood believe that a person acquired the trade of pimping to avoid the natural occurrences that go on in an inner-city neighborhood. They *believe* that a pimp is using a protective custody sort of occupation by keeping women in his surroundings, instead of hood niggas. But I must say that those who are under that impression are wrong. What they fail to realize is this: pimping is not a course that is taken at a college or university, then after graduation, one hits the streets with his newfound career, and takes it from there.

Just about every black pimp there is in the United States shared the same surroundings during his upbringing as any gangbanger, drug dealer, stick-up kid, and drug addict. The only thing is his occupation is viewed by the underprivileged as "overprivileged." And that reason alone will always have another man looking for a reason to knock it. Dislike can come out of anybody, but envy and jealousy is usually driven by one's own misfortunes and insecurity.

Any man who is sure of himself and satisfied with his lifestyle wouldn't give two fucks about the next man's occupation. It is always some nigga with issues who's in denial of other people's success. Their focus is always on something that revolves around the media or entertainment industry, instead of worrying about their own life.

And the funny thing about it is this here: if one of those same types of dudes with the "a pimp id a soft nigga" mentality were to be approached by a gorgeous woman of any race who's a prostitute, and she says something like,

"Listen, I sell my body for a living. I need somebody to hold me down and take care of me. I'll do all the work and give you all of the money. I'm really not too good at handling things when it comes to the money. I make about $1,500 a day, and I have $700 on me now that I made so far today. If you can hold me down, I'll go out and make the rest, and just give you the $700 now!"

Now I'm willing to bet a thousand dollars to a wooden nickel that 99.9 percent of hood niggas will not let that opportunity pass them by. And when they accept it, all the thoughts that they would usually entertain to knock a pimp for what he does, they'll try to see themselves as an exception, especially with the "I'm still a gangsta," or "tough nigga", mentally.

Who's to say that three out of every four pimps, who have been pimps for a while, don't feel that exact same way at heart, and through actions when necessary? A lot of people who are in denial of the existence of pimps think that anyone who considers himself a pimp is some clown type of dude who is caught up in a fad. They will continue to be in denial even if they were to witness him live and direct in action, with his "working prostitutes" present. They'll think of him as someone who is "trying to pimp," instead of actually pimping.

They'll say to themselves that "there is no way this guy can actually be making a living off of that pimp shit." It is somewhat understood why a person would not put it past somebody as being caught up in a fad. Several things that people live and die for are adopted by the media, then used for the purpose of entertainment. Once that occurs, it soon becomes a fad.

There was a time when bandannas and pants sagging was strictly a dress code for active gang affiliates. That style has now been acquired by any and everyone who feels like sporting it. So the fad trend, as far as a pimp is concerned, only helped cater to the thoughts of those who were already in denial of the concept. Many "hood" type of individuals that can be found in inner city neighborhoods and/or jails and prisons are quick to take offense to someone who is noticed as a pimp in their presence. Reason being, most of these fellas grew up living what would be considered a "hard life." As far as they're concerned, they've "been through everything."

Shootouts. Being shot. Killings. Prison. Drug dealing. Drug using. Stabbing. Fights. Funerals. Taking losses, etc., etc., etc. They feel that when it comes to the minority's underworld, there's nothing they're not familiar with.

However, a pimp in their presence reminds them that there is something that goes on in the minority's underworld that they're not "honestly" familiar with. And the more serious that a pimp takes his career, either by heart, success, or both, the more offended people will feel by his presence.

Do not mistake this book as a glorification of the lifestyle of pimps and prostitutes. Or is it an encouragement to influence someone to take interest in the life. The purpose is to help the misunderstood understand. The only thing that blockbuster hits and TV shows has to offer are the "Huggy Bear," "Baby Powders," "Money Mikes," and "Gay Man Pimps." What I have to offer is the real thing!

Everything in this book is not expected to be agreed upon by everybody who comes in contact with it. That's all right though. Neither is everything in the Holy Bible, agreed upon, and that book has much more of a greater purpose than many other books ever written throughout the beginning of mankind. And let me not forget to mention this in regard to the women. In the "Prostitute" section of this book, I speak solely upon those which matters apply to. There are absolutely no intentions to demoralize or degrade women. Women are a very appreciated beings. And without the existence of their presence, the world would not be as it is.

Furthermore, every woman will not experience the things mentioned in this book. The things mentioned are not "earthly" matters; they are "pimp and prostitute" matters. Some may be able to relate to some of the matters partially, while others may be able to relate to some in whole. Some may be able to familiarize themselves with one matter or other only by witnessing or knowing what someone else goes through. And some may not be able to identify any further than the contents of this book. Whatever the case is, appreciate it for being real.

While it's some people's fantasy, it's other people's reality. While it's some people's past, it's other people's present, and will become someone's future. The art of prostitution, along with the later-revolutionized concept of pimping, has been here many generations before us, and will remain here long after us. There is nothing that will ever bring about a change through one's sensitivity, or the alternatives they use to cover it up such as, humor, entertainment, or discouragement.

A person's sex life has always been the first thing that they're recognized by from those who are aware of it. That is the way of the world. For those who are disturbed by pimp, prostitutes, or both, to whatever degree, they should be satisfied with the fact that they don't indulge and not give so much thought to something that doesn't pertain to them.

Unlike drugs, sex isn't an element that has been taken from the earth and has been manipulated by the intelligence of man into a substance used for mind-altering substances. It is rather a natural "birth-given right" that adults consensually exercise at their discretion, whether they get paid for it or not.

Made in the USA
San Bernardino, CA
09 August 2013